One Sip at a Time

One Sip at a Time

Learning to Live in Provence

Keith Van Sickle

Published by Dresher Publishing, Menlo Park, California. Printed in the United States

ISBN 978-0-9983120-0-2

First Edition

Cover design by Teddi Black
Map by Sally Dexter
Illustrations by Anthony Genilo

To Val, my partner in all things

Je t'aimais, je t'aime et je t'aimerai

ALSO BY KEITH VAN SICKLE

Table of Contents

Prologue

Part One

Prologue

"*Monsieur, vous êtes dans ma voiture!*"

Wait a minute, what did she say?

I had just gotten into my car and before I could even put on my seat belt, this lady was rapping on my window.

I couldn't understand what she was saying but I could tell she was mad. Maybe it was because of her clenched jaw. Or the way she was glaring at me. And she sure was squeezing the heck out of that purse.

All I knew was, This Is Not Good.

I was in a parking lot in Provence, in southern France, where my wife Val and I would be staying for the next three months. We had picked up our rental car just the day before and were still stocking the house with supplies. My French, not very good to begin with, was rusty and I struggled to understand what this lady was saying.

"*Monsieur, vous êtes dans ma voiture!*" she said again, this time even louder. I struggled to make sense of the words, especially with her strong *Provençal* accent.

Slowly it came to me. "Sir, you are in my car!"

What??

I looked around and saw her pack of cigarettes on the dashboard, then my own car two spaces away. Oh my god, it was true! Our cars were similar and we had used our keys to remotely unlock them at the same time. I had seen her car's lights flash and assumed it was mine.

"*Excusez-moi madame,*" I stammered. "*Je suis...*" Dang, what was the word for sorry? Ah yes, "*desolé.*" I carefully got out and continued apologizing while she looked at me suspiciously. After all, what idiot doesn't know his own car?

This wasn't the first time I had done something stupid and been unable to explain myself. And it wouldn't be the last. That's what happens when you live in another country and haven't yet mastered the language.

So...how did I get here?

It had all started years earlier. One day, to my surprise, my company offered me a job in Switzerland. Wait, the land of chocolate and cuckoo clocks? Where they speak four languages but none of them is English? Why would I leave sunny California to live in a country famous for snow?

Sometimes crazy opportunities come along and you just have to go for it. Val and I decided this was one of those, so she looked for a job in Switzerland and miraculously found one near mine. Two months later we were off to the canton of Neuchâtel, in the French-speaking part of the country.

It changed our lives.

We lived in a village so small that the streets did not have names and the cows outnumbered the people. The only traffic jams were when a farmer was moving his herd from a field on one side of the road to the other.

We learned to follow the rules and be precise, because the Swiss are nothing if not orderly. Even today I can't stand to be a minute late for a meeting.

And we learned to appreciate wine. The people in our village had been making it for more than a thousand years, so wine became a natural part of every dinner. And just across the border were the famous wines of France and Italy, which we eagerly explored.

Stores in Switzerland closed at noon on Saturday and didn't open again until Monday, which bugged us at first. We worked all week, which meant we had to cram our shopping into Saturday morning. What a pain!

But eventually we came to appreciate everything being closed. We *couldn't* shop, we *couldn't* run errands. So we did what everyone else did– enjoyed the weekend as a time for family and friends, a time for hikes in the mountains and lunches in the garden.

Living in Switzerland was so different from what we were used to in Silicon Valley. People worked hard just like at home, but life was somehow less hectic. Work wasn't the be-all and end-all: Val was once eating a sandwich at her desk when a colleague came by and lectured her on the importance of taking a proper lunch break.

And everyone took all of their vacation days; not to do so was considered unhealthy.

We took advantage of Switzerland's central location to travel all over Europe, visiting towns big and small with our dog in tow. So much history! We loved exploring the various cultures, with their traditional foods and local customs.

Everywhere we went we could see that the way people lived was not like back home. They spent so much time together having a glass of wine in a café, or sharing a long, multi-course meal, and the focus seemed to be on enjoying life. Could this be the *joie de vivre* we had always heard about? We began to try it ourselves.

Overseas postings don't last forever, and after five too-short years our Swiss adventure ended and we headed home. As we said our goodbyes, we realized that we had never fully integrated into Switzerland, and the primary reason was because we couldn't communicate well. We had learned to speak some French, but not enough. Val became conversational–barely–while I only learned a few words. That was a big regret.

We loved being back in California. We could see our friends and families and enjoy local favorites like tacos and bagels, but boy did we miss Europe. It was like there had been an extra dimension to our lives that had disappeared. Couldn't we live there again?

Expat assignments are rare and, despite our best efforts, no opportunities came along. And our jobs kept us busy–I had joined a startup and Val traveled a lot for work.

Years went by. But the itch to live in Europe didn't go away. So finally we decided to do something even crazier than moving to Switzerland. We would invent our own expat gig.

We quit our jobs (that was scary) and started consulting. We figured we could work mostly in California, but be away for a few months at a time and communicate via email and Skype. We would be part-time expats! Or at least we would try it and see if it worked.

We decided to go to Provence, a place we had always liked. It was warmer and less expensive than Switzerland and the food was great.

We couldn't wait to experience that *joie de vivre* again.

That just left the language. The French are famous for *not* speaking English. We were determined to do better than we had in Switzerland, and if we wanted to truly experience France we would need to speak French.

We have always liked a challenge and this would be a good one: figuring out not only the French language but also the French themselves, so unlike Americans. If we could really understand their culture, their way of living, their quirks and foibles...how great that would be.

We looked for a place to rent and found a good one an hour north of Marseille. It was a refurbished farmhouse outside the village of Mollégès, with a big backyard for our dog Lucca.

Three months in Provence! We dreamed of fitting in and eventually going native, cooking *daube de boeuf* and sipping fine Burgundy late into the night. Maybe Val would become *Valérie*, with that cute little accent mark.

Our village was small, with a downtown barely a block long, but it had all the basic services. Pascal, the owner of our house, had grown up nearby and shared his local knowledge with us. He told us where to find the baker with the best *pain au chocolat* and the butcher who still used his grandmother's sausage recipe.

It was so good to be back. We went to outdoor markets practically every day, buying delicious fruits and breads and cheeses. We worked off all our big meals by getting bikes and puffing our way through the countryside, past vineyards and olive groves and the occasional shepherd watching over his flock.

We puzzled our way through the daily newspaper, dictionary in hand, and took a language class to improve our vocabulary. And while we stayed on top of our consulting work, it's fair to say that more than once a glass of wine took precedence over a spreadsheet.

We closely observed the French in their native habitat, noting the ways they were different from us. Their driving etiquette, for example. Or their strange obsession with Nutella. Or the custom of greeting one another with kisses, with its secret code of who kissed whom and how many times.

Even though we tried, we did not get to know anyone well. It would be a stretch to claim that we became friends with Pascal and his partner Claire, though they did invite us to their place for drinks a couple of times and once we had them over for dinner. So that was a start.

And while my French language skills remained pathetic, I slowly made progress and was motivated to do the hard work to get better.

As our trip ended and we flew home, we talked about the following year. Should we do it again?

Absolutely!

My Provence

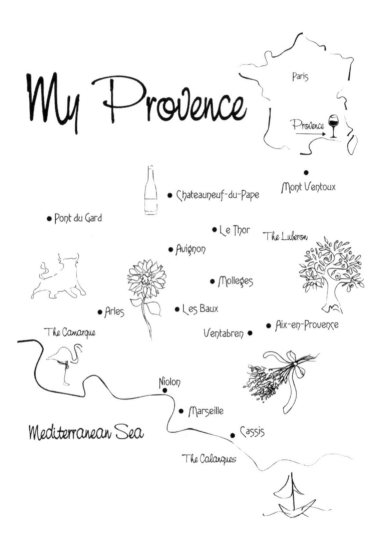

Paris

Provence

Mont Ventoux

Chateauneuf-du-Pape

Pont du Gard

Le Thor

The Luberon

Avignon

Molleges

Arles

Les Baux

Aix-en-Provence

Ventabren

Niolon

Mediterranean Sea

Marseille

Cassis

The Camargue

The Calanques

Part One

A Chilly Beginning

After months of planning and anticipation, our second French adventure began in late March. We flew from San Francisco to Frankfurt, picked up our car and headed south.

It wasn't the easiest way to get to Provence but we needed a direct flight because of Lucca. It's all about the dog.

Tired from jet lag, we didn't drive very far, but we made sure to at least cross the border out of Germany. There's something about that first meal in France that's magical.

We made it to Montbéliard, a town in the far north of the country, and dropped Lucca off at our hotel. It was dark and cold when we arrived – the last day of winter – but a hearty meal of *confit de canard* warmed us right up. Now we could drive back to the hotel for some much-needed sleep.

Think again!

When we got to where we had left our car, we found the underground parking lot shut tight behind a huge metal gate. What the heck? There was a sign next to it, in French of course, that took us a while to decipher.

We finally figured out that the lot had closed at 8pm(?!) and that we needed to see the police in order to get our car out. So we resigned ourselves to finding the police station.

We had to ask several passers-by before we were finally directed on a long walk to the far side of town. Off we trudged, shivering all the way. This was certainly not the delightful first night in France that we had envisioned.

We got to the station and haltingly explained our situation. We thought we had been understood, but when they told us to sit in the hallway and wait, we weren't so sure. The hallway was unheated and before long our toes were numb.

After waiting a half hour we decided to try again. This time a new set of officers was behind the desk. Aha! We realized that there had been a shift change in progress. The old shift wanted to stick the new shift with those Americans who spoke such bad French.

We were asked to fill out a stack of forms (the French love paperwork) and then an officer gave us a card that would open a special door to the parking lot. His complicated directions included multiple turns and a store with a striped awning, then a hidden stairway. But we weren't sure because he spoke so quickly.

Our stunned expressions must have made him take pity on us. Or else there were no crimes in progress because the next thing we knew we were in a squad car with three of Montbéliard's finest.

When we got to the parking lot, the officers showed us the hidden stairway and the special door. Of course, it was easy to find if you knew where to look.

What an adventure! But at least we didn't have to pay for parking.

Driving in French

The next morning we got up early, stuffed ourselves with warm and flaky croissants, and hit the road. We had a long drive ahead but would be in Provence by nightfall–we smiled just thinking about it. Then I looked around, saw all the cars with French license plates, and shuddered.

The French road system is excellent. The country is covered by a comprehensive network of *autoroutes* – similar to our Interstate Highway System–along with plenty of secondary roads. They are in uniformly good condition and are well-marked so you can find your way. If there is any downside to the French road system it would have to be...French drivers.

The French like to drive much too fast. No

matter what road you are on or how fast you are driving, you can be sure that a French driver will be tailgating you. I think it is required by law. You could be setting a new land speed record at the Bonneville Salt Flats and if you looked in your rearview mirror you would see a French driver just inches from your tailpipe.

In fact, it is possible that French drivers own all the land speed records, how could they not? It's just that after setting them they stopped for lunch and a nap and forgot to call the people at Guinness to make it official.

After tailgating you for a while, the French driver will finally decide to pass you. There are two basic ways to do this: on a nice, roomy *autoroute* or on a narrow, winding country road.

On the *autoroute*, the obvious thing is for the other car to move one lane to the left in order to pass you. But no, there's no challenge in that. Instead, the preferred method is to pass you *in your own lane.* This means zooming by so closely that you can tell if the other driver had onions for lunch. And it requires that you, the one being passed by this insane guy, drive perfectly straight. Anything that might cause your car to move even a millimeter to the left – a cough, a sneeze, a fart – could result in a fiery death.

On the narrow, winding roads, by contrast, the French driver doesn't do anything so silly as try to pass while close to you. No, no, it is much better to move as far to the left as possible so as to be able to terrorize oncoming traffic, careening back into your lane only at the last possible instant. Ah, the thrill! The *grandeur!*

And then there's the stopping. Even in situations where it would be incredibly dangerous to stop – say, in a traffic circle or the middle of an intersection – French drivers will frequently stop, look at the road signs, discuss which way they should go, have a smoke, and maybe talk about last night's soccer game, before finally moving along again.

In other words: If you care at all about safety, take the train.

Springtime in Provence

We reached our rental house just before sundown. It was outside the hilltop village of Ventabren, near Aix-en-Provence. We had decided to stay further east in Provence than last time, to explore new sights and see if we liked one place better than the other.

Our house sat near a cliff that looked out over a valley, with Ventabren in the distance. It was the first day of spring, still chilly, and we dreamed of the warmer days to come. We imagined ourselves sitting on our terrace, glasses of rosé in hand, watching the sky change color as evening fell.

We were welcomed by the caretakers, Jean-Claude and Dominique, who showed us around the house and explained how everything worked. They told us where to find their favorite butcher and favorite vegetable market, but argued about who was the best baker. We promised to check out each of their favorites and let them know which we liked best.

Jean-Claude spoke English so our conversation was a mix of French and English. We hoped to make enough progress to make it all French by the end of our stay.

We liked everything about the house except that it had a nasty smell. Jean-Claude suggested that maybe the house was just musty after being closed up for the winter. We agreed to air it out and see if that fixed the problem.

It didn't, but that's another story.

A True French Dog

Soon after we arrived, we went for a hike around the *Étang de Berre*, a bay so large that it's almost an inland sea. We sat on a bench to eat our lunch and a little poodle came up to me, looking for a handout.

I had finished my sandwich and was eating an apple. I figured that since Lucca liked apples this poodle would too, so I tossed him a piece.

Obviously, I had not counted on the refined palates of French dogs. He sniffed the apple and gave me a withering look. Then he turned his back, heisted his leg over the apple, and trotted away.

Will Someone Please Talk to Me?

One of our big goals, especially for me, was to speak better French. Val's had gotten pretty good but mine remained rudimentary, despite our last stay in France and the language classes I had taken in California.

The best way to learn a language is to talk to people. But how could I find a French person with the patience to talk to someone like me, a beginner?

A friend had pointed us to a website where you could find "language partners." The idea was to help someone learn your language while they, in turn, helped you learn theirs.

Before we came to France, I had posted an entry on the website, explaining my interests and the name of the town where we would be staying. I got one reply, from a fellow named Étienne, a retired Parisian banker who had moved to Provence for the weather.He was an avid gardener and amateur beekeeper and wanted to learn English to keep his mind busy.

Étienne and I began meeting weekly at his nearby house. Well, almost weekly. He cancelled once because a swarm of rogue bees had invaded the neighborhood.He was a member of the local bee society's Emergency Response Team and had to go corral them.

Étienne and I would talk for an hour or so, first in French and then in English. Our levels were about the same and each of us was patient as the other stumbled along. He loved to talk economics and politics, as do I, and I could tell that I was starting to improve my French. His wife Brigitte was a warm and outgoing lady who became Val's language partner, an unexpected bonus.

I also met Odile, a retired postal worker, through a language school in Aix-en-Provence. She was easy to talk to and an endless source of local expressions. Though sometimes she would point out that one I had picked up on my own "really isn't for polite company."

After we had been in Provence for a couple

of weeks, someone finally responded to Val's posting. It was Viviane, a teacher at the local international high school, and she invited us to meet her for coffee in Aix. Our dance card was getting full!

First French Friends

We met Viviane in Aix and it must have gone well because she invited us to her house the following Sunday afternoon for coffee. We expected it to be an hour or so in French and English.

We were wrong.

We got to Viviane's house in the early afternoon and met her husband Gérard and their six-year-old son André. Then a neighbor wandered over to meet the Americans. No one spoke English except Viviane, so it was all in French.

After a while we sat down for coffee and Gérard joined us. He was a funny guy who loved to tell jokes so he told a couple, which we kind of understood. Or at least we laughed when we were supposed to.

Then Gérard decided it was our turn to tell a joke, so he and Viviane looked at us expectantly, smiles on their faces. Uh oh.

I knew I was in trouble. You see, Val doesn't like to tell jokes–that's my specialty. So as Viviane and Gérard looked at the two of us, Val turned to me as well. Now they were all three looking at me and smiling, waiting.

I could feel myself start to panic. Then I thought, "Calm down, Keith. These are nice people, they've welcomed you into their home and they know you are making an effort to learn their language. Don't worry about making mistakes, just do your best."

So I took a deep breath and stammered out an old joke about a farmer and his truck. Or at least I tried to, because when I got to the punch line I realized there was a key word I didn't know how to say. Luckily, Val bailed me out, everyone laughed and Gérard gave me a pat on the shoulder. Maybe they were just being polite but I felt pretty darned good.

After about an hour, Val and I figured we should head home so the family could enjoy their weekend. We were starting to say our goodbyes when Viviane jumped up and said, "You can't leave yet, I baked a cake!" So cake it was, then they wanted to show us some family photo albums, and more time went by.

At this point we thought we really should get out of their hair so we started our goodbyes again. But then Gérard's father dropped in and wanted to chat with us.

He was a fascinating guy. He told us that he had been a professional photographer, just like his father and grandfather and just like Gérard. Quite the family business! They had a studio with nearly a million negatives going back more than a century, to the early days of photography.

By now it was late afternoon, the traditional time for an *aperitif,* one of our favorite French customs. It usually consisted of something simple, just a drink with snacks like olives or nuts or sometimes sardines. It was a great way to ease into dinner.

Gérard went to get a bottle of pastis while Viviane smeared little toasts with the delicious

Provençal spread called *tapenade,* made from chopped olives and anchovies. Of course we couldn't leave yet. So we ate and drank and talked as the sun got lower in the sky.

It was almost dark by the time we finally headed out. Our visit had been fun, relaxed, friendly – and all in French. Somehow, our hour spent over coffee had turned into a long, wonderful afternoon. We felt like we had crossed some important but invisible barrier along the road to understanding France.

The Bread of Life

"Should we stop and get bread?"

It was a dilemma.

It was always like this when it came to bread. There were just too many things to think about.

We were passing our favorite *boulangerie, Gout de Pain*, the one that Dominique had recommended. It was a longish drive from our place so we didn't go there every day. But we were coming back from a hike and it was on the way.

"If we get bread tonight, it won't be fresh for breakfast," I said. "Maybe we should skip it now and I'll go to Madame Cantillon's *boulangerie* in the morning."

"That works for breakfast but we will still need fresh bread later in the day for when our guests arrive," Val pointed out. "And you can't get fresh bread from Madame Cantillon in the afternoon because she takes a four hour lunch."

French bread is wonderful. It doesn't stay fresh for long but nothing compares to just-baked French bread. It comes in every shape and size imaginable, baked with all kinds of ingredients, with seeds on the outside, with fruit inside, with nuts, with olives, you name it. We found that even the smallest *boulangerie* would have at least half a dozen kinds of baguette, plus a variety of loaves.

And there were *boulangeries* everywhere, sometimes right across the street from each other. They coordinated their schedules so that they didn't have the same days off during the week or the same vacations. Can you imagine a village with no fresh bread? Revolutions have been started over less!

There were so many decisions to make. What kind of bread to get? How many? On Sunday mornings we would see long lines at the *boulangeries* as everyone stocked up for the big Sunday lunch. We saw people carrying bread on the street all the time, sometimes breaking off the end of a baguette (the *crouton*) for a snack on the way home.

And then there was the slicing question. Did you have it sliced by the bakery or slice it yourself? A good bread knife is an absolute kitchen essential, right up there with a corkscrew.

Did you slice a baguette sideways, into little disks, so people could spread *tapenade* on them? Did you slice it lengthwise, like for breakfast–half a baguette with butter and jam is a *tartine*, the way many French people start their day. Or did you just follow the French family tradition of letting each person tear off a hunk for themselves?

Val and I finally agreed that we would get fresh bread for dinner from *Gout de Pain*, toast the leftovers for breakfast in the morning, and get fresh bread from the *Intermarché* supermarket in the afternoon. That seemed like the best solution.

But then again, maybe we should get croissants...

Plumbing the Depths

The bad *odeurs* in our house did not go away.

First we tried airing out the house. That was challenging because the weather was below freezing at night. We did our best but it didn't help, so Jean-Claude called in the plumbers.

They arrived the next day and banged on pipes for a while. Then they announced that the problem was because our roof vent was of an insufficient height. Roof vent? Apparently the sewer line had a vent out to the roof but it wasn't high enough. We had smelled gas escaping from the sewer line.

That was definitely something we didn't want to smell.

So the next day the plumbers extended our vent pipe way above the roof. It proudly towered over all our neighbors' vents. We thought maybe we should tie a pirate flag to it.

But the bad smells still did not go away.

Then we had good and bad news. The bad news was that we had guests for the weekend and had to explain why the house occasionally stank. But the good news was that one of our guests was an engineer and he figured out what was going on.

It turned out that the house had an American dishwasher, which was unusual in France. It was much bigger than the typical French model and so powerful that when it drained, the water coming out overwhelmed the standard French U-joint (a plumbing fixture) that it was connected to.

This blasted all the water out of the U-joint and created a path for sewer smells to enter the house. So every time we used the dishwasher, it caused the house to stink until we happened to run water in the sink, which refilled the joint and blocked the smells.

In other words, the problem was caused by France and the United States not working well together. Hmm, probably not a first.

Luckily, this one was easy to fix. The plumbers came in, swapped out the U-joint and the problem was solved. Even better, the owner of the house felt so bad about the inconvenience that he sent us two nice bottles of wine.

French Fjords

Our Swiss friends Béatrice and Alexandre came to stay with us, which gave us the opportunity to visit Cassis. Alexandre wanted to have their famous Mediterranean fish soup, *soupe de poisson*.

The port of Cassis sits just below Cap Canaille, the highest sea cliff in France, and the town is surrounded by vineyards that come almost to the water's edge. As we drove in, we could see sailboats gently rocking in the harbor, bathed in the clear sunlight that has seduced so many painters. Magical.

It seemed we weren't the only ones with the idea of visiting Cassis. It was Victory Day, one of the four (yes, four) national holidays in May. With so many visitors, parking was a disaster. We went to lot after lot, getting more and more frustrated.

Finally, we found a spot where a car was about

to leave. We were waiting for it when another car zipped in front of us at the last second. The guy wouldn't move so we had to content ourselves with hurling French insults at him.

Val was remarkably skillful, I must say. I was pleased with my own cutting and witty insult until Alexandre pointed out that I needed to work on my pronunciation. Apparently I had called him a "large duck."

We eventually found a parking space and had our *soupe* at the port, then went on a boat tour of the *calanques*. These are narrow, rocky inlets surrounded by towering limestone cliffs, kind of like craggy fjords. They are popular with boaters and sunbathers, and the contrast between the grey of the cliffs and the deep blue waters of the Med makes them especially striking.

On the drive home, Alexandre wanted to prepare me for the next time someone stole my parking place. So he taught some new *gros mots*, the kind of words you should never use in front of your mother.

They would definitely come in handy!

Joyeux Anniversaire

It was Val's birthday so we went to a restaurant in Arles that Jean-Claude had recommended. It was the first organic restaurant in France to get a Michelin star and had since been awarded a second. We got the *"menu surprise"* of seven courses, each one a mystery until it arrived at the table.

Luckily, it was not the season for sheep brains or other icky things so there were no unpleasant surprises. The chef used lots of vegetables, some from his garden, and combined many different flavors. Each course was so beautiful that Val said it was like a work of art that you enjoyed twice, once by looking at it and again by eating it.

Each course was matched with a specially selected wine. The last was a "mystery wine" that we were supposed to try and identify. It was a dessert wine in a black glass so we couldn't even tell if it was red or white.

We don't drink a lot of sweet wines so we were stumped. It turned out to be a Rivesaltes. Ah, but of course! That was our next guess!

The chef had written a cookbook and I bought one for Val, which he signed for her. He was obviously smitten, but then who wouldn't be? His inscription read, "*Valérie, vous êtes jeune et délicieuse comme les fèves du printemps, Gilles*" ("Valerie, you are young and delicious like the fava beans of springtime, Gilles").

I had so much to learn from the French.

Lunch All Afternoon

After hesitating for a few weeks, we finally gathered our courage and invited Jean-Claude and Dominique and their kids for lunch. Val was nervous about preparing a meal for a gourmet like Jean-Claude.

But she needn't have worried. The food was delicious, as always, and everyone loved it. The three bottles of wine might have helped. And the view from our terrace across to Ventabren was glorious.

Our guests showed up at noon and stayed until...almost dinnertime. We had heard that French lunches could go on for a while, but all afternoon?

I'm not sure how we managed to speak French for that long. Luckily, everyone liked to talk about food and wine, two topics beloved in France. Where did you get your fennel? How did you prepare the lamb? What do you think of the latest vintage? Is it true that Americans eat hamburgers every day?

Val did most of the talking for us but I chipped in from time to time. Even if my brain couldn't work fast enough to form complete sentences, I was thrilled that I could mostly follow the conversation.

We felt a real sense of accomplishment as the meal ended and we waved goodbye to our guests. Yes, we had successfully managed a long lunch. But it was more than that.

We really liked Jean-Claude and Dominique and they seemed to like us. Our conversation had been downright warm! We felt like we had made a connection that was more than superficial; it was the beginning of friendship.

We had taken another step along our path to understanding France.

Shooting the Rapids

I knew we were in trouble when Val said I should steer.

We were going canoeing and every time we've ever canoed, the conversation has gone like this:

Me: "Who should steer?"

Val: "You should steer."

Me: "Are you sure?"

Val: "Yes, you should steer."

Me: "Ok, I'll steer."

Then we get in the canoe and within five minutes Val is overcome by a mad lust for power and starts to steer. Which means we are both steering. So we flip the canoe. Happens every time.

But Val promised to be good so we got our oars and listened to the safety lecture. Unfortunately, it was in French and the guy spoke really fast, so I had trouble understanding him. But I was sure I heard "death," "drowning" and "painful."

He slowed down at the end so we would be certain to understand him. I could have sworn he said, "Be sure that only one person steers the canoe or you could suffer a *painful death* by *drowning*." At this point I was petrified.

But off we went. The route went from Fontaine-de-Vaucluse, where a powerful underground river bursts to the surface, to L'Isle-sur-la-Sorgue.

We were told that there would be a Class 23 rapid, which made me nervous. In the United States, our 1-to-5 rating system stops with Class 5 rapids, those steep, violent chutes meant only for experts. What horrors could Class 23 have in store for us?

Then I found out that the French classification system is different from ours. Class 23 is actually quite mild. The formal description is, "It is advised that each person consume no more than a half-bottle of wine before embarking."

As promised, Val let me steer. So I guess I have to take responsibility for that unfortunate episode with the low-hanging branches. And those fishermen weren't too happy when we drifted to the wrong side of the river and tangled up their lines. But I digress.

The route was a simple one, from point A to point B, and rivers only go one direction. So I'm still not sure how we managed to get lost. But we eventually realized we were entering a storm drain and furiously paddled backwards while a group of picnickers laughed at us. From then on we both paid attention and got to the end without further mishaps.

Next time I'm letting Val steer.

Ups and Downs

We were in St.-Rémy and stopped at one of our favorite restaurants for lunch. I went to the restroom, a one-room affair used by both men and women, and had to wait in line behind four ladies.

When I finally made it into the restroom I was surprised to find the toilet seat up. Even after four ladies! I told Val about this and she said it was common, that even when there was a separate ladies room, women would often leave the toilet seat up after they were done. Apparently it's a French custom.

I love this country.

Taking a Risk

We went for a hike and I was in charge of making the sandwiches. Val had gotten some ham because she wanted a ham sandwich. It's funny, because she never eats them in the US but loves them in France.

I asked if she wanted butter or mustard and she looked at me like I was an idiot. "Butter, of course."

"But I thought you liked mustard on your ham sandwiches," I protested.

"That's in Switzerland. The Swiss put mustard on their ham sandwiches. But we're in France and the French use butter."

I had never noticed the sandwich change when we crossed the Franco-Swiss border. I knew some of the other changes – "*dîner*" means dinner in France but lunch in Switzerland, and freeway signs are blue in France and green in Switzerland – but the whole mustard/butter thing was news to me.

Far be it from me to complain. Val was queen of the kitchen. So I meekly asked, "What kind?"

That stumped her. You see, we always kept at least two in the house. I liked sweet butter while Val preferred the kind they make in Brittany, with big grains of salt mixed in.

In France, you can't have too many choices when it comes to food. Besides the butters, at any one time we had seven or eight cheeses and as many wines as I could get my hands on. De Gaulle once said that it was hard to be president of the fractious French because, "how can you govern a country which has 246 varieties of cheese?"

Anyway, Val told me to use salty butter but I suspected that officially, a French ham sandwich should be made with sweet. We were probably breaking the French Sandwich Regulations. Plus, she told me to put lettuce on hers, which was definitely not French. Only a *Californienne* would do something so gauche.

I imagined what would happen to us on our hike. We'd be out on some lovely trail in the middle of nowhere. Suddenly, we'd come to a checkpoint manned by the Sandwich Police, who would be randomly pulling aside hikers to check their lunches. *Quelle horreur*, they would pick me!

"Excuse me, *monsieur*, can you please come this way?" I'd start to get nervous. "Can you please open your backpack?" Sweat would start to trickle down my forehead. "Hmm, two sandwiches wrapped in foil. Can you please open... that one?"

Thank god! He'd picked the one with the proper sweet butter. Ok, we're in the clear! But then his long, Gallic nose would start to twitch. His finely honed sandwich instincts would tell him that something was amiss.

"*Monsieur*, we have to be very careful to uphold the law. I must ask you to open the other sandwich as well." I would be trapped. Val would slowly sidle up the hiking trail, preparing to make a run for it. I would unwrap the sandwich. Immediately, the inspector would know that he was dealing with a sandwich criminal.

"What is this?!" he would cry. "Ham with... salty butter? And...*sacré bleu*...lettuce? Off with his head!"

Thank goodness this didn't actually happen. But I decided that next time maybe we should go with salami.

Our Version of Immersion

We felt like we passed a milestone when we had a (nearly) all-French-language day. It started with lunch and shopping in Aix, followed by reading the newspaper at a café before going to the movies.

The film was "OSS 117," a parody of James Bond, and very funny. The humor was broad enough and the plot so simple that we could enjoy it even if we didn't understand every word.

After the movie we went over to Jean-Claude's house to pay the rent. This led, as usual, to a discussion of food and wine. Jean-Claude always seemed to have a new tip on a restaurant or a winery that we should check out.

That evening we had dinner with Étienne and Brigitte. They had invited us along with some other friends of theirs, a total of five couples. It would be all in French.

I was intimidated by the thought of going to

my first big French dinner party. I had managed to survive one-on-one conversations and meals with just me and Val and another couple. But this would be ten people at once.

The French consider dinner conversation to be a national art form and everyone is expected to participate. I had visions of our dinner being like one of those French movies where erudite people sit around discussing postmodern philosophy and quoting Molière. My hands got sweaty just thinking about it.

Happily, everyone was friendly and down to earth. And they were curious about life in the United States, which gave us something safe to talk about.

During the dinner, I was proud of myself for jumping in and expounding on a subject I know something about. I held the table spellbound with my erudite description of French versus California wines. I talked about types of grapes, fermentation techniques, the use of oak barrels.

Or at least that's what I thought I said. From the puzzled looks I got, I could tell that my French still needed some work.

How to Kiss a Frenchman

Viviane, Gérard and André came over for lunch one Saturday. It was a long meal with plenty of courses and plenty of wine, something we were starting to get used to. When they left, Gérard gave me a kiss on each cheek.

People kiss each other all the time in France, as they do in Switzerland, but the rules can vary and we were never sure which set was in play.

The Swiss, as you would expect, are very orderly. Three kisses on the cheeks, left-right-left, no exceptions. People shake hands when they are first introduced but move to kisses as they get to know each other. Women kiss women, women kiss men and men kiss women. Men exchange firm and manly handshakes.

There are clear rules that keep everyone organized. They were probably printed in our village handbook when we lived in Switzerland, right next to the phone numbers for the fire department and the fondue delivery service.

In France it gets more complicated and it varies by region. In Paris it is two kisses. The Parisians also start with the right cheek rather than the left and men don't kiss each other. Parisian men carry man purses, sure, but kissing each other would be a bit much.

When we had stayed in Provence the year before we had started to get into the kissing program. We had discovered that it was three kisses like in Switzerland but the cheek sequence was right-left-right rather than left-right-left. *It is very important to keep this straight.* One of our Swiss friends once had an awkward moment with a French woman. He went left, she went right, and he ended up kissing her on the lips. Quite the international incident.

The other thing about Provence is that men kiss each other. Not all men, but men who are good friends – "*potes.*" The year before, our landlord Pascal gave me the full three-kiss treatment when we left at the end of our stay. I thought it was a warm and friendly gesture but maybe he was just glad to be rid of me.

Here, not far from where we had stayed the year before, it was two kisses rather than three. How were we supposed to know this? Was there a border we had crossed but somehow missed the sign? ("Welcome to Eastern Provence. Please Follow the Local Kissing Regulations. And Enjoy Your Lunch, Especially the Asparagus, Which is Delicious Right Now.")

If you gave three kisses when it should be two, would people think you were rather pushy and forward? If you only gave two kisses instead of three, would you be considered standoffish?

One thing that was consistent across Provence was that men kissed each other. So when Gérard kissed me I wasn't shocked. But I was worried that I might mix up the left-right sequence like my Swiss friend and give him a real kiss. Good thing that didn't happen because Gérard really loved his garlic!

French Enthusiasm

Most French road signs are easy to understand.
But this one always mystified me.

I saw it all over. What could it mean?

– 20% off *crêpes suzette!*
– New Yves Saint Laurent fashions now
   available!
– National holiday today!
– National strike today!

It's a mystery.

Bêê Bêê Black Sheep

We went to a local *transhumance* festival one day. This is where sheep parade through town before being driven to up to the mountains, where they graze in cooler pastures for the summer. It would have been nice if they had left a few weeks earlier because the temperature was close to 100.

It was supposed to start with the herding dogs demonstrating their skills. Some sheep were in a pen and the idea was to let them out and then have the dogs herd them back.

The sheep were released onto one end of the main street and started running through town. Unfortunately, no one had thought to block off the other end of the street. The town was so small that in no time the sheep had raced up the street and scattered out into the countryside, with the dogs chasing after them. The dogs certainly got a good workout but there wasn't much to see.

While we waited, a group in traditional dress marched through town on stilts. I'm not sure why they were on stilts but it might have had something to do with all the sheep droppings.

Finally, the escapees were rounded up and the parade began. Hundreds of sheep were driven through town, herded by the dogs. Not something you see very often back in California.

Then we went home and had lamb chops for dinner.

Testosterone Shortage?

It happened every time.

Val likes her coffee strong. I like mine with milk. So when we would get coffee, Val would order a *café serré*, which is an extra-strong espresso. I would order a *noisette*, which is regular espresso with milk added. It comes in a cute little glass.

Sometimes the person who delivered the coffee would not be the one who took the order. And this being France, the lady always gets her drink first. The waiter would assume that Val had ordered the *noisette* because, presumably, it's a ladies drink.

"*Votre noisette, madame?*" they would ask and Val would start to smirk. She would sit up straighter, nod her head towards me and say, "*Non. C'est le café de monsieur.*" Then she would give me a pitying look.

Ok fine, FINE. I like milk in my coffee, is that a crime? It wasn't like I had ordered a Shirley Temple, for goodness sake. Though you'd never know it by the way people acted.

The waiter would then turn to me and, with a sneer, throw down my *noisette.* I could see his lips move. No doubt, he was muttering "girly man" in French.

Onky Tonk Woman

We went to a concert featuring Viviane's band. Everyone in it was a high school teacher and they sang a mix of French and English songs.

They did a couple of Rolling Stones numbers, including Honky Tonk Woman. But I wasn't sure it was the best choice because the French have trouble pronouncing the letter "h." So it came out more like "Onky Tonk Woman." It was like the trouble the French have with "th," which was why my name Keith was usually pronounced "Kees."

You think, what's so hard about an "h" sound or a "th" sound? Any kid can do it. But that's the key – if you don't learn some sounds as a kid, you never really learn them. There's a "u" sound in French, in words like *bu*, that I could never get right. One of my French teachers described it as like making an "o" with your lips but an "e" with your mouth. Good luck with that.

Another tough one is the French "r" sound, which is made in the back of the throat. It's a little like gargling. The American "r" is much different – we make it in the mouth. Trying to think about how sounds are made, and adjusting your tongue, lips and throat while you speak, is pretty much impossible.

I was talking to a French person once about the nearby town of Arles, which I pronounced as an American-style "Arl." Wrong! Every time I said it, he gave me that confused-dog look, cocking his head like he was thinking, "He's trying to communicate with me, I wonder what he's saying."

Meanwhile, I was thinking, "What's wrong with this guy? Everybody knows Arles!" So I kept repeating it over and over, pronouncing it with a more and more distinct American "r" ("Arrrl!... Arrrrrrrrl!!") which only made it worse.

Finally he said, "Oh, you mean *Arles!*" with a perfect French "r," and I felt like a complete moron. So a singer who couldn't pronounce his "h" shouldn't have surprised me. In fact, the next morning I found myself singing "Onky Tonk Woman" in the shower!

Abandoned in Provence

Val had to travel for business so it was Lucca and me all alone. Given my trial by fire while she was gone, I felt like I had begun to make real progress in French.

The first test was to get a haircut. This was something I definitely didn't want to get wrong. Happily, I was able to tell the *coiffeuse* what I wanted and I seemed to have communicated reasonably well (though I did not let Val take any pictures until my hair grew out a little.)

Then I had a long conversation with Étienne. I explained my views on Turkey's potential entry into the European Union. Surprisingly, he agreed, which meant either I did a good job or he felt sorry for me.

The next day I saw the latest Star Trek movie and learned how to say, "Live long and prosper" in French. "*Longue vie et prosperité*" will certainly come in handy at cocktail parties.

And Lucca responded well to everything I said in French, though I think the only things he ever heard were "Let's play fetch" and "Time for dinner."

I also read the newspaper every day and finished a short novel I had been working my way through. So my French was definitely improving. There are so many frustrations in learning a new language, and so much drudgery, that it was satisfying to feel things start to come together.

Living Dangerously

Whenever we needed some excitement in our lives, we would drive through the nearby town of La Fare-les-Oliviers. We had to take its main road if we wanted to go anywhere west of our house, so we found ourselves there all the time. It may be the most hair-raising driving in France.

As far as I could tell, some traffic engineer had come up with an insidious plan to terrorize drivers. It was like a recipe:

– Take a narrow, two-lane French road.
– Use one of the lanes for parking so there is even   less room for cars.
– Add a sidewalk so narrow that pedestrians have to walk in the street.
– In addition to the heavy auto traffic and all the pedestrians in the street, make it a favorite road for cyclists so there will always be lots of bikes darting in and out.
– Add a major intersection.

– But no stoplight.

– Or even a stop sign.

And *voilà!* Bumper cars *à la Française!*

"S" For $400 Please

We went for a hike in the Aiguebrun Valley, one of France's hidden gems. It is well off the beaten track, between Lourmarin and Bonnieux, at the end of a winding road. The valley is beautiful, bordered by sheer cliffs and covered with a forest of deep green pine trees.

As we drove through the valley's only town of Buoux, we debated how to pronounce it. Was it "Boo-oh" or "Boo-oxe"? It wasn't clear if we should pronounce the final "x."

In general, if a French word ends with a final, single consonant, that consonant is not pronounced. But this being France, there were always exceptions, and especially regional ones.

In Provence, people tend to pronounce the last letter. So *mas*, the word for a large traditional *Provençal* house, is pronounced "mas." Which made us think that "Boo-oxe" was the way to go.

But then there were the nearby towns of Velaux and Coudoux. You pronounced the "x" in Coudoux but not in Velaux, even though it was right next door. What's up with that?

We were having dinner with Pascal one night and I asked him how to pronounce Carpentras, the nearby home of France's biggest truffle market. He told me that people there used to pronounce the final "s" but no longer, "only the old guys."

As we were finishing dinner, I mentioned that I wanted go to the Carpentras truffle market someday and when I said "Carpentras" I accidentally pronounced the "s." Pascal shot me a hard look and said, "I'm not that old yet, pal."

The Root of All Evil

The French political spectrum is well to the left of ours. Your typical Democrat, for example, would be considered conservative by French standards. France has a large Socialist Party and France's leading newspaper, *Le Monde*, falls into the socialist camp.

I had first noticed this when the financial crisis hit the US. The tone of their editorials had been sneering, along the lines of, "Nya nya nya, we told you that your capitalist system stinks." (Of course, when the crisis hit France shortly after, the tone changed abruptly to, "*Ayayaïe!* Save us!")

I liked to buy *Le Monde* on Saturday so I could get the weekly magazine. This often had long, interesting articles. But I started to notice a distinctive tone. Kind of like: Money Is Bad.

One week I read an article titled, "The New

Face of Poverty in America." It showed heart-wrenching photos of people who were living in terrible circumstances.

Later there was an article about Brits in financial trouble. A few years earlier the pound sterling had been sky-high, making housing in France seem cheap. British retirees took advantage of this to buy big places in France and live like royalty.

But recently the pound had crashed, making it unaffordable for these poor people. Plus the lack of good bangers and mash in France was causing them untold human misery.

So thousands of retirees were selling their homes and moving back to Jolly Olde England.

The most recent article was on the trials and tribulations of a family that had won millions in France's national lottery. I read all about the grasping relatives, jealous neighbors, fears of kidnapping, and other terrible, terrible things that happen when you are rich.

These unfortunate people had somehow found the strength to buy a mansion on the Riviera where I was sure they were suffering still.

As far as I could tell, the attitude of *Le Monde* was:

- If you don't have money, it's bad.
- If you used to have money but don't any more, it's worse.
- If you have lots of money, *quelle catastrophe!*

I looked forward to the next article, where I imagined we would learn that money causes baldness.

Counterfeit Melon

The French take their melons seriously. And the best are the famous *melons de Cavaillon*. The people of Cavaillon are so proud that they have erected a giant melon statue at the entrance to the city.

It was melon season and we ate them all the time. And, in the proper French fashion, we became very picky.

One day we were at a restaurant where I ordered melon and prosciutto as a starter. When it arrived, something didn't look...quite right. Time to test out my French.

"This is *melon de Cavaillon*, isn't it?" I asked suspiciously.

The waiter started shuffling his feet nervously.

"I...I'm sorry, *monsieur*," he stammered, "our supplier made a mistake today and brought melons from the Languedoc. But I assure you that they are delicious."

I poked at the melon, cut off a piece, sniffed it. It seemed perfectly fine but, let's be honest, it was not a *melon de Cavaillon.* "We'll see," I said, and glowered at the waiter as he scurried off.

You can bet that we wouldn't eat at this restaurant again. If the chef didn't use the proper ingredients for a simple melon dish, who knew what he would put in his *coq au vin?*

Vive la Différence!

Viviane called and she sounded desperate.

She explained that she and a group of fellow business teachers would be working in England during the summer. This would allow them to learn how companies there operate. But first they wanted to have some idea of what they were getting into.

Viviane had arranged to have one of her neighbors, a Brit working in France, come and talk to the teachers about what it was like to work for an English company. But he had dropped out at the last minute. The meeting was in three days and Viviane needed us to substitute.

We gently explained that while we shared a common language, we had never worked in England. No matter, she said, you know about Anglo-Saxon companies and that's what's important.

Anglo-Saxon?

It turns out that the French use this term to describe American-style business practices. It is shorthand for what we might call free-market capitalism. In France, this is definitely not a compliment.

It is true that Val and I understand American capitalism. Coming from the wild west of the Silicon Valley, we understand it in one of its more extreme forms.

So we agreed to make a presentation, explaining some of the differences between working for a French company and an American one. Luckily, all of the teachers taught at *International Baccalaureate* schools so we would be able to do it in English.

Then we did what anyone does to become an expert on short notice – we used Google. And we called some French friends in California who gave us a quick tutorial. Then we boiled our research down to a few key points.

Most were not surprising. For example, French companies are more formal than American ones, especially in terms of dress code and hierarchy. Business suits may be fading away on our side of the Atlantic (I can't remember the last time I wore one) but they are still common in France. And while you might greet the president of an American company with a casual, "Hi, Bob," that would be shocking in France. No, in France it is always, *"Bonjour, Monsieur le President."*

We learned that Americans are generally more risk-taking. We change jobs more often and it is not a scary thing to join a startup company (well, not too scary). By contrast, it would be a major risk to join one in France. If it failed, as startups often do, it would be a black mark that could follow you for the rest of your career.

Similarly, American companies are more risk-taking. If a company sees an attractive business opportunity, it is more likely to invest and hire and go for it. If things work out, the company grows and new jobs are created. And if things don't work out, the company can cut its losses by downsizing, as painful as that is.

In France, by contrast, it is extremely difficult and expensive to downsize. So companies are less likely to hire in the first place.

The most surprising thing we learned was

that there is much more mixing of professional and personal lives in France. In the US, we might have lunch with our colleagues or the occasional drink after work, but that would be about it. Mostly we keep our home and work lives separate.

By contrast, when you arrive at work in France you shake hands and say hello to each person in the office. You spend a half hour chatting at the coffee machine before starting your workday. You see your colleagues socially on the weekends and even go on vacation together!

When I think about some of the people I've worked with, then imagine us vacationing together, my head hurts.

The big day arrived and we met Viviane in a conference room at her school. She introduced us to her colleagues, who seemed nervous at the prospect of taking a trip all the way across the English Channel.

We began by giving some background on ourselves and our careers. We talked about having worked in different companies, in a variety of industries. We described our jobs in areas like finance, marketing, and human resources.

This turned out to be a showstopper. Apparently, it is uncommon in France to move around as much as we have. This led to a long discussion of why and how we had done this and whether it would even be possible in France.

Then we gave our presentation and the teachers asked questions. The discussion got heated on the subject of companies pursuing growth but taking the risk of having to downsize. No one likes layoffs and the French have a history of violent action opposing them.

One teacher asked us, pointedly, how the Anglo-Saxon system could *possibly* be superior to the French one. We didn't think it was a good idea to start an international incident so we fell back on our experience of living in Switzerland. In other words, we stayed neutral. We pointed out that each system has its advantages and disadvantages and then quickly moved on to another subject.

In the end, the teachers appreciated our presentation and felt better prepared for their summer abroad. And we felt like we had gained a little insight into the role of work in French people's lives.

Best of all, after the meeting Viviane rewarded us with lunch at a restaurant that had a nice long wine list.

The French Citizenship Test

We had croissants for breakfast and as usual we made a mess. They were so flaky that there were crumbs everywhere – on our shirts, the table, the floor, the dog.

But when French people ate croissants there was never a crumb in sight. How did they do it?

Did they have specially-evolved types of teeth? Were they taught proper crumb-prevention techniques in elementary school? We thought maybe we should invite some of our friends over for brunch and film them with a hidden camera to discover the secret.

This got me to thinking that maybe you had to master proper croissant eating to become a

French citizen. I imagined it being part of the rigorous French Citizenship Exam, a multi-day affair.

The first day would be French language, where you would have to write an essay using all 26 (yes, 26) tenses of French verbs.

The second day would be French cultural appreciation, where you would watch a French film and explain what happened. This would be tricky because nothing ever actually happens in French films. You would get extra points for including references to *Man's Fate* or existentialism.

The third day would be French food, where you would be required to match dozens of cheeses with the correct wines, a challenge that even the French would find daunting.

The fourth day would be the driving test, where you would have to find a parking place in Paris in under an hour. Points would be deducted if you ever used your turn signal, something real *Parisiens* never do.

Finally, if you passed all of these tests, you would get to the final exam. They would bring you into a small room and seat you at a table covered with special, highly sensitive crumb detectors.

Then a member of the French Immigration Service would bring you the lightest, flakiest croissant imaginable and say, with a menacing smile, "*Bon appétit!*"

Hearts and Minds

There was an election for the European parliament during our stay. A few nights before it, each of the major parties had a televised rally to fire up the troops and get out the vote. We figured that watching the rallies would give us insight into the important political issues of the day. Plus it would be good for our French.

Most of the speeches were boring, with the usual applause lines. There were shout-outs to dignitaries in the audience, potshots at the competition, promises to lead France boldly into the future. The crowd would clap politely but there wasn't a lot of real enthusiasm.

Then things got exciting at the rally of the conservative party. The final speaker was wrapping up his speech and wanted to go out on a high note.

"We will work together with the European Union on common initiatives like the electric car," he thundered, "but we will defend ourselves against the bureaucrats in Brussels when it comes to important French interests like"...(dramatic pause)..."RAW MILK CHEESE!"

The crowd went wild, cheering and stamping their feet, throwing things in the air. It was like Charles de Gaulle had just liberated Paris from the Nazis or something.

Val turned to me. "Did he really say *raw milk cheese?*" she asked. "Whoa!"

The next day we asked Brigitte and Étienne about this. It's true, they told us, and they were outraged. They explained that there was a move afoot to force cheese makers across Europe to pasteurize their milk. "This will make the cheese tasteless!" they cried. "Tasteless food – the English must be behind it!"

Sometimes it is in the most unlikely places that you find what really moves French hearts.

A few days later the results came in and the conservative party was the big winner. They far outperformed the pre-election polls.

Never underestimate the power of cheese.

Answering the Call of Nature

It was a beautiful day so we went for a bike ride. I had had a little too much coffee so after a while I stopped by the side of the road to do my business.

This is common in France. Every day we would pass cars stopped by the side of the road. The man would be answering the call of nature while the woman would sit inside, pretending she didn't know the guy standing next to her car taking a *pipi*.

Is this a great country, or what?

Back-to-School Night

We went to a lecture at the Archival Center For the French Overseas Territories. A professor was discussing her work called *The Indigenous Peoples and Their Metamorphoses: A History of The Repressive Imperial French Regime.*

What were we thinking? I wasn't sure I would understand this presentation in English, much less French. But Val thought we needed the language practice so off we went.

The professor talked for an hour, moving her glasses from the end of her nose to the top of her head and back again, rubbing her eyes, tapping her papers for emphasis, and periodically departing from her prepared remarks to go off on long tangents. What I understood was basically this: colonialism bad, human rights good. There might have been some other important points in all those words but I think this pretty much sums it up.

The best part was the Q&A. The moderator kept telling the students in the audience, "Don't be shy! Ask a question!" But as soon as they tried, one of the other professors in the audience would butt in and go on and on *and on* about THEIR research and how critical IT was. One guy told us three separate times about his vitally important research until finally people started to walk out.

My favorite was the professor sitting next to us, with a perfect combination of the "academic look" and the "French look." He had unkempt grey hair (academic), a black turtleneck (French) under a tweed jacket (academic), stylish shoes (French), small, round, black-rimmed glasses (definitely French) and he didn't seem to have bathed in days (uh, let's call that academic.)

This guy kept making flattering remarks to the presenter – I think he was trying to hit on her. I hoped he would compare her to a fava bean but I guess that's a pickup line that only French chefs use.

France's Worst Off-Ramp

We were driving on the freeway and saw a backup in the right lane at least a half-mile long. But of course! It was the *Jas de Bouffan* off-ramp, one that we avoided like the plague.

When you exited at *Jas de Bouffan*, the off-ramp took you to a major intersection. You were forced to go either left or right, but there was no stoplight. Instead there were two lanes of traffic roaring by in each direction.

If you wanted to turn right, it was dangerous but doable. The real problem was if you wanted to turn left. How the heck did you cross so many lanes of busy traffic?

Normally, a road designer would manage this in one of several ways. In the US, with so much space, we use a lot of cloverleaf designs. In Europe, where cities are more compact, a traffic circle is usually used. Or you can have a stoplight. Even the humble stop sign will do the job.

But no, none of these 20th-century technologies, or even one from the 19th century, was good enough for the brainiac who designed this off-ramp. Instead, he took an even older approach: Survival of the Fittest.

At *Jas de Bouffan*, each driver who wanted to turn left had to wait until there was a rare gap in traffic coming from the left. Then he had to quickly make sure there was also a gap in the busy traffic coming from the right. Then he had to go like hell.

Of course, the cars on the road knew this. And no one wanted to be the wimp that let someone from the freeway cut in. So as drivers approached the intersection they sped up and crowded the car in front to make sure there was no daylight between them. It was a festival of French driving machismo.

And the backup on the freeway got longer and longer.

Eventually, a tiny gap would appear. At this point the driver waiting at the front of the off-ramp would be desperate. He would launch himself across the road like a missile, followed closely by a line of cars behind him. This would result in a riot of squealing tires, slammed brakes, honking horns and very bad words. It was a recipe for accidents, and we had seen our share.

But why in the world was the off-ramp designed this way?

- Out of a desire to add excitement to the humdrum lives of commuters?
- Because the freeway budget got cut when funds were diverted to the Glories of Escargot museum?
- Because *someone* had to graduate last in their class from the National Off-Ramp Design Academy?

Personally, I thought it demonstrated – this being Provence and all – that pastis and freeway design *just don't mix.*

Explosions of Flavor

We celebrated our 20th wedding anniversary at the end of May. When I took Val to Paris for our honeymoon – her first trip to France–little did I know that it would lead to a lifelong love affair with the country.

We decided to try a famous local restaurant for our anniversary dinner. It specialized in so-called molecular cuisine, with dishes like transparent ravioli and "popcorn cocaine."

Our waiter was too-cool-for-school, with spiky hair that pointed in all directions. Back in college, my friend Jon used to shower at night and then go to bed with wet hair. When he woke up it was completely wacky like our waiter's, but it wasn't considered fashionable back then.

Rather than order a bottle of wine, we ordered wines by the glass that had been selected to go with the food. The sommelier came over and explained each before he poured it. In French, of course.

Unfortunately, he was rather pompous and gave completely ridiculous descriptions. I couldn't help myself – I had to have a little fun with him. Val wasn't happy to see that I had made good progress with the language.

For one wine, when the sommelier said it would be, "like an explosion of flavor in your mouth," I looked alarmed. "Explosion?" I said. "Is it dangerous?" He wasn't amused and haughtily informed me that I would be safe.

When the next wine came, the sommelier told us how feminine it was. That made me worried that it might be a risk to my masculinity, so I asked if it was safe for a man to drink it. He was annoyed but said yes, it would be ok.

The next wine was delivered with a flowery description so long that it almost put me to sleep. The sommelier finished by saying that we would feel a little "pop" on the end of our tongue. That perked me up.

Val could tell what I was thinking and gave me a firm look that meant, "Don't say it, buster," but I went ahead anyway.

"There's not going to be another explosion, is there?" I asked. "I think that first wine broke a couple of teeth!"

The sommelier didn't know what to say so he just poured the wine and left. We never saw him again.

Snack Time

We went to the movies and I checked out the snack bar. Most of the stuff was the same as back home, like popcorn, M&M's, and ice cream. But there was one I had never seen before: cotton candy in a box.

In France, cotton candy is called *"barbe à papa,"* or "papa's beard." Which makes perfect sense if dad's whiskers happen to be day-glo pink or neon blue.

This particular treat was labeled *"Barbe à Boîte"* – "Beard in a Box." Hmm, this definitely fell into the category of Bad Product Names. It would need some serious marketing help if it hoped to crack the US market.

Reading Pagnol in Provence

I fell in love with Marcel Pagnol during our stay. This author, director and playwright, best known in the United States for films like "Jean de Florette," was one of the artistic giants of 20th-century France. I found his books surprisingly easy to read and finished a couple during our stay.

Pagnol was from Provence and most of his work is set there, so he holds a special place in the hearts of the *Provençaux*. They love his books and films because they are about themselves – their language, their land, their customs. When I would mention Pagnol, people would smile and quote to me from his films...which were made in the 1930s!

But it is not just people in Provence who love Pagnol. His books are widely read in French schools. A friend who is in his 50s told me that for people his age, *La Gloire de Mon Père* was the first "grownup" book they read in school and so it had special meaning for them.

The French educational system is standardized, with a national curriculum that all French students follow. This means that in addition to reading books by Pagnol, every French student reads books like The Three Musketeers and *Les Miserables*. These are important books about France, by French authors, and reading them creates a shared cultural patrimony.

When some Swiss friends visited us, we asked if there was anything like this in Switzerland. Of course not, they told us. We can't even agree on one national language, much less a common reading list! And the US, with its decentralized educational system, doesn't have anything like it either.

Val and I tried to figure out if there were American books that fit the bill – classic works by great authors, describing our common American heritage. We thought of books like Huck Finn and The Grapes of Wrath, but not everyone reads them. For people my age, the best I could come up with in terms of common cultural experiences were movies like The Wizard of Oz and television shows like M*A*S*H.

This was yet another of the many differences between France and America – Jean Valjean versus the Cowardly Lion – that were so much fun to explore.

Heading Home

Before we knew it, it was the middle of June and time to go home. We started the long drive north to Frankfurt and talked about how our trip had gone.

Of course we had had a great time. Springtime in France–what's not to like? It was cold at the beginning but the days got progressively longer and warmer and flowers bloomed everywhere. Each week the markets had more ripe fruits and vegetables. There's a reason people flock to Provence.

We were also tired. Stepping out of your routine and exploring another way of living takes a considerable effort. It is scary, exciting...and worth it.

As for the language, we had both improved, especially me. After months of being surrounded by French, I could now mostly understand what people were saying.

And sometimes I could even respond! Though it took me a few moments to translate my thoughts into French, conjugate the verbs and decide whether the nouns were masculine or feminine. At which point the conversation had usually moved on.

Having the ability to communicate, as limited as it was, meant we could connect with people in a way we never could in Switzerland. Sometimes it was as simple as being able to order bread at the *boulangerie*, not just point at what you wanted. Or understanding a waiter when he described the day's special.

Most important, we could carry on mealtime conversations. Being able to participate in that most sacred of French rituals meant we could make friends. And by understanding French people, real people like us but with a different outlook on life, we could begin to understand France.

So we headed home, looking forward to the familiar comforts of our American life but already eager to return to France the next year.

Interregnum

Our next trip didn't happen as we had hoped it would, with unexpected family responsibilities keeping us close to home for the next few years. We were able to take vacations to see our French friends, and stayed in touch via the occasional email, but our dream of living part-time in Provence had to be put on hold.

We were surprised by how much we missed France. After all, we had only been there for a couple of long stays. But there were so many things we missed.

We missed the constant presence of history, like when we would walk past an ancient fountain on the way to the store. And our bike rides through the vineyards, with their leafy vines growing under the warm sun of Provence. And, of course, the long meals with their endless discussions over food and wine.

France had started to capture our hearts. It wasn't just a place we visited; it was becoming one of the places we lived.

Thomas Jefferson is supposed to have said, "Every man has two countries – his own and France." Maybe he was on to something.

While in California, we maintained our "French connection" as best we could. Val joined a conversation group and I took an online course. We started hanging out at a French café and went to the artsy movie theater whenever a French import hit town. And we found ourselves spending more time with friends with whom we shared a love of France.

But nothing could replace being in *la belle France* itself.

Finally, things came together so that we could spend another springtime there. We decided to check out a new town, further north in Provence but close enough that we could still see our friends.

We made arrangements with our clients to work from afar, bought our plane tickets and packed our bags. We couldn't wait to be back!

Part Two

Monks in the Garden

As we had done before, we flew from San Francisco to Frankfurt so Lucca could have a direct flight. Then we picked up our car and drove to France.

We spent the night in the Alsace region, near Strasbourg. After a dinner of *tarte flambé* and a bottle of Pinot Blanc, we knew that we had really, truly, finally made it back to France. All was right with the world.

The next day we drove to Beaune, a medieval walled city in the heart of Burgundy. We saw the sights and, most importantly, visited a wine shop to pick up a few bottles. A well-stocked *cave* is an essential part of French living and we wanted to start filling ours right away.

The next day we continued our drive south and arrived at our rental home late in the afternoon. It was in Le Thor, a small town located midway between the papal city of Avignon and L'Isle-sur-la-Sorgue, famous for having the largest outdoor market in France.

Rather than a house, this time we would be staying in a monastery built in the 1500s, with stone walls nearly two feet thick. We heard rumors that monks were buried behind the monastery but I'm happy to say we never found any in our garden.

After being abandoned for years, the monastery had been sold to a developer, who divided it into several units surrounding the central courtyard. Luckily, they had been remodeled since the days of the monks and had all the modern conveniences.

The monastery was at the end of a long, private road lined with plane trees. They were leafless at the moment, the end of March, but we expected them to fill out soon and provide welcome shade in the warmer days to come.

Our next-door neighbors, Pierre and Fabienne,

were friendly and we did our best to chat with them in French. It was only a short walk to the center of town and Fabienne told us about a path that kept us off the busy main street. It ran beside the old city walls, across a footbridge and along a river where we would often see ducks and fishermen.

After a turn that took us past Le Thor's 12th-century church, we reached the *boulangerie*, reputed to be the best in the region. The route was so pleasant that we started walking into town most mornings, for a breakfast of coffee and a croissant, or to buy fresh bread, and of course on Saturday for the local market.

We seemed to have found another comfortable place to stay and felt well "installed," as the French say. We hoped we would be able to find language partners, to improve our French and maybe make new friends.

Sex Discrimination

We tried the language exchange website again but this time our postings got no response. Maybe Le Thor was too small?

Then Val had the bright idea of contacting the tourist office. By happy coincidence, a woman from town had dropped by just the day before, inquiring after any Anglo-Saxons who could help her with English. Perfect!

This is how we met Sophie, who lived just blocks away. She and her husband had moved to Provence when he took early retirement. Sophie was a wealth of local knowledge, pointing us to the best places to get fresh vegetables, eggs, you name it.

She also invited us to join her weekly exercise class, which is how I found myself the only man in a room full of middle-aged ladies. We were doing leg kicks and the teacher kept barking something at us that sounded like "allaylayfee."

What the heck was she saying? Sometimes French words just sort of ran together in my head. Maybe we were doing something wrong? No one seemed upset but she sure was shouting.

Finally I figured it out. She was encouraging us with the French version of "Let's go, girls!"

Wait, was that sex discrimination?

Take Two Comprimé and Call Me in the Morning

The weather was cold and rainy and I woke up with a runny nose. Time to go to the pharmacy.

In the US, I can go to a drugstore or grocery store to get what I need. But no, not in France. Dangerous substances like cold medicines are strictly controlled and can only be dispensed by pharmacies.

The French love their pharmacies and they are everywhere. Even a little town like Le Thor had three of them, and two were right across the street from each other. In the cities, pharmacies are like Starbucks in the US, with one on practically every corner.

In France, not only do you have to go to a pharmacy to get simple over-the-counter medicines, you are even prevented from just grabbing what you want and paying for it. Instead, you have to stand in line and wait to discuss your medical issue with a licensed pharmacist. And everyone behind you in line gets to listen in.

When your vocabulary is limited and prone to errors like mine, the conversation goes like this:

Me: Do you have the American
                product called Nyquil?
Pharmacist: You are in France.
Me: Right, ok, do you have any
                French cold medicine?
Pharmacist: You should use this one, you
                put it up your nose.
Me: Um, I don't want to put any-
                thing up my nose.
Pharmacist: Well, what do you want then?
Me: Do you have any cold medicine
                that comes in fur?
Pharmacist: ???
Val: He means pills.

(I had confused the words for pill and fur, which are similar).

Me: I mean do you have cold medi-
                cine that comes in pills?

Pharmacist: Ah. Here. I hope these make
                you better so you won't be
                back.

I was curious as to what other dangerous substances needed to be controlled by a licensed pharmacist, so I looked behind the counter. Let's see: Eye drops...aspirin...Vaseline...

The French clearly have higher safety standards than we do in the US.

I was happy to see that mouthwash was not yet a controlled substance. Good thing, because I really didn't want to have a discussion with a pharmacist about how to make my breath fresh and minty.

Drinking With the Enemy

Fabienne and Pierre invited us over for an *aperitif* shortly after we arrived, along with our neighbors Marie-France and Xavier. We hadn't met them yet because they had been away when we moved in.

We hit it off right away. Xavier and Marie-France were retired antique dealers who had traveled the world in search of rare and beautiful treasures. We also love to travel and so we swapped stories of foreign adventures.

When Marie-France talked about traveling to India after college, she mentioned something that made me think she had been a student in the late 1960's. So I took a risk and asked if she and Xavier were *soixante-huitards*.

This is someone who had been involved in the student uprisings of 1968 that shook France and almost brought down the government. I had read the word in an article that morning and by some miracle it came to mind at exactly the right moment.

Marie-France and Xavier both smiled and sat up straighter and kind of glowed, happily acknowledging that they were indeed *soixante-huitards*. In France it is a badge of honor, a mark of having been at the center of the counter-cultural revolution.

The American equivalent might be someone who had been there when Jimi Hendrix rocked Woodstock. But without all the mud.

Being proud veterans of the famous student revolt meant that our new neighbors were probably Socialists. And we knew from the portrait of Charles de Gaulle staring sternly down at us that Fabienne and Pierre were staunch conservatives.

It was good to see that people with such widely divergent political views could also be good neighbors, happily sharing a bottle of wine and a bowl of olives.

And the Winner Is...

The French presidential election took place that spring and it was interesting to follow. I was eager to see how France was different from the US. We were able to follow the entire campaign because it was only six weeks long.

Wait, six weeks? Ok, that's a big difference right there.

The French actually vote for president twice. First is a month of campaigning by candidates from at least a dozen political parties, followed by a vote. The top two winners face off two weeks later.

As expected, the finalists were incumbent president Nicolas Sarkozy from the Conservative Party, known to all as Sarko, and François Hollande from the Socialist Party. The vote was expected to be close.

Hollande came into the race with some major liabilities. He wasn't his party's first choice and only became their candidate after favorite Dominique Strauss-Kahn was arrested in New York for attempted rape. That's a story in itself.

Hollande was criticized for inexperience, having never held national office or even been mayor of a major city. And he was so indecisive that his nickname was *"Monsieur Flanby"* because he wobbled like that popular brand of custard.

But he had one trump card. He wasn't Sarko.

Yes, Sarko was wildly unpopular. He was elected right before the global financial meltdown and was somehow blamed for it. Ok, that was unfair.

But Sarko hadn't helped himself by flaunting his taste for the finer things in life, like expensive watches, dinners at top restaurants, and yachting vacations with his rich buddies. This was dumb to do during a deep recession and had earned him the nickname "President Bling Bling." Many French couldn't stand the guy.

Hollande was smart. His campaign strategy consisted mostly of him running around saying, "I will be a normal president" (i.e., not a jerk like you-know-who). This turned out to be very effective and he built a lead in the polls that looked hard to overcome.

It all came down to the grand finale, a debate where the candidates faced each other across a small table. Sarko and Hollande went at it for two hours in a kind of steel-cage death match. They thrust, they parried, they mocked, they sneered. I didn't understand everything but the body language told me a lot. Not only was it great political theater, it was a chance to see French verbal combat at its finest.

Sarko was aggressive, knowing he had to deliver a knockout blow. But it didn't work. Voters weren't crazy about Hollande but it turns out that they really, really disliked Sarko.

So Hollande became President of France and I was surprised to learn that this also made him Prince of Andorra, the only elected monarch in the world.

Prince Hollande? In the US we sometimes complain about an "imperial presidency" but in France it was true!

A Special French Lesson

A small taste of *Provençal* hospitality...

We went to Sophie's house for a language exchange. We had started meeting one morning a week at our house and one morning at hers, each time for a couple of hours. Or so we thought.

This time Sophie's husband Jacques joined us. First we got a tour of his sculpture garden–he's a retired engineer and a self-taught sculptor and had an upcoming exhibition. Sophie served chocolates and cookies to go with a choice of coffee or juice, while Jacques kept talking about how much he *loved* champagne.

When our lesson ended, we were getting ready to go when Jacques disappeared for a moment and came back with four glasses of champagne. What could we say but yes? And who doesn't love champagne? Especially when it came from a winery where Jacques sometimes helped out at harvest time.

When the bottle was drained, Sophie invited us to join them for a lunch of pasta with her homemade tomato sauce, while Jacques raided the *cave* for a well-aged Chateauneuf-du-Pape. We ate on the terrace, warmed by the early spring sun. Next came a platter of five cheeses that they happened to have in the kitchen. Doesn't everyone?

When we finished, it was time for coffee and more chocolate, at which point it was late afternoon. We waddled home with yet another bottle of wine that Jacques had presented to us as a gift.

All in all, it was a very long lesson, not only in French but also in *joie de vivre*. How we love this part of the world! And we seemed to be making some new friends.

Auntie Em!

We had a *mistral* that lasted four days and each day it had gotten stronger. This is the fierce, gusty wind of Provence that clears out everything in its path

We'd heard about the *mistral* but never really experienced its full effects before. So we foolishly decided that our back patio was sheltered enough from the elements that it would be ok to eat lunch outside.

Have you ever seen a sudden gust of wind pick up an entire salad and leave you with a big empty bowl? I can now say that I have.

After lunch I watched the *mistral* force a couple of birds to crash land in our back yard. They lay on the ground for a moment, stunned and blinking, before slowly taking off again.

And I could have sworn I saw the neighbor's cat fly by.

Tighter and Whiter

We were driving through town and there was someone up ahead dressed in a t-shirt and white pants. As soon as Val spotted him she started to eagerly lean forward. Then we got closer and saw that it was a painter on his way home for lunch. His pants were dirty and a little saggy. Val slumped back in her seat. "They need to be tighter and whiter," she grumbled.

Yes, it was *Course Camarguaise* season, where young men in their tight white pants try to pull various doodads off a bull's horns without getting gored. I don't know if Val cares much for the bulls but she sure loves those tight white pants.

Course Camarguaise is a variation on bullfighting,

but in France the bulls don't get hurt. In fact, the best ones become celebrities and some even have endorsement deals. Many of the nearby towns had arenas built specially for the sport, with big dirt fields surrounded by low fences.

In preparation for a *Course*, the bulls have ribbons, strings and little pompons attached to their horns, each one worth a certain number of points. I don't know who puts them on but I certainly wouldn't want that job. The *raseteurs* then have to run up to the bull and try to pull them off.

The usual strategy is to approach the bull from behind, then grab at the horns, race for the nearest fence, and leap over it to safety. This usually works but once in a while the bull decides to jump over the fence after the *raseteur*, at which point all hell breaks loose.

It's a sport that requires a lot of sprinting and a love of danger, so the *raseteurs* tend to be young men. And the traditional costume is white shirt and pants, the tighter the better.

It's a lot of fun and we went whenever we could. Val would scan the papers daily to see if there was a *Course* nearby. And she always made sure to sit in the front row, eagerly leaning forward as the young men entered the ring.

Spectacular Views

After being in Le Thor for a few weeks, we received a second response to our online posting looking for language partners. That's when Thérèse, an elementary school teacher in a town nearby, replied and asked if we would like to meet. After several emails back and forth she invited us to her house for Sunday lunch.

We were welcomed that day by Thérèse, her husband Yves and their two college-aged kids, Juliette and Marius, plus Marius's girlfriend Nicole. I'm not sure if Nicole really wanted to meet the Americans or just came because Thérèse is an excellent cook.

The meal had course after course – Sunday lunch is France's big meal of the week–and gave us a chance to get to know each other. We spoke mostly in French. The conversation was stiff at the start but it warmed up as we went, helped by a glass or two of wine. Or maybe it was three or four.

After we finished lunch we thought we should head home but Yves had other ideas. He invited us to join them for a drive out in the country. Yves hadn't had any wine so we were happy to let him drive. Plus he was a professional truck driver and knew all the best routes.

We took a winding little road to Crillon-le-Brave, a hilltop village with views in all directions. To the north we could see Mont Ventoux, topped by the huge field of white rocks that makes it appear snow-capped all year long. To the east was the *Dentelles de Montmirail*, a craggy rock formation that towers over the wine village of Gigondas. Everywhere we looked were spectacular views.

It was late when we got back to the house and said our goodbyes. We had enjoyed a memorable afternoon and, better yet, felt like we had begun new friendships.

Maybe people who are open to new languages are also open to new people? We had certainly been lucky so far.

A Bite Too Far

It was Fabienne's birthday and she was kind enough to invite us to her party. Because it was May Day, a holiday, the dozen or so guests had time for a leisurely lunch.

Fabienne and Pierre had set up tables in the monastery's courtyard, with brightly-colored tablecloths and umbrellas to keep the sun off our heads. We hoped our French would be good enough for us to get by.

The party started with champagne and appetizers–many, many little toasts with foie gras and fig jam.

Then came the first course, a vegetable terrine with tomato sauce, accompanied by deviled eggs. The food gave everyone a powerful thirst that we quenched with large quantities of chilled rosé wine. It slid down your throat so easily you didn't notice how much you were drinking. At least not yet.

After that was Basque chicken and lots more wine. It was really good but we were getting full.

Ok, time to fire up the grill! Pierre cooked two enormous platters of lamb brochettes and spicy *merguez* sausage, which we somehow polished off. Plus more wine, now moving to red.

There's a concept from Normandy called the *trou normand*, the "Norman hole" that helps you when you are full. You drink a fiery brandy that supposedly burns a hole through the food in your stomach and allows you to eat more. Everyone was stuffed at this point so Pierre brought out a bottle of *eau de vie* and down the hatch it went.

Occasionally, one of the guests would serenade us with Edith Piaf songs. Her voice was so beautiful that we guessed she had once been a professional singer. We would all stop to listen to her. Then we would go back to eating. I wished she would sing more often so I could take a break.

Uh oh, what was Pierre doing back at the grill? Were those really fat Toulouse sausages? They are delicious but...oh my. Somehow we managed to each have one. With bread and wine, of course.

Then it was time for the cheese course. Everyone was required to have at least three "morsels." With bread and wine. At this point I was wishing I had a second stomach.

Finally it was time for dessert. The end was in sight! Fabienne carried out a chocolate cake, so scrumptious-looking that I actually started to get hungry again. And luckily, there was no bread this time. I resolved to start tapering back on the wine.

Then another birthday cake appeared. Two?? Plus champagne, of course. So much for the tapering back.

From time to time, I would try to chat with the people sitting near me but they all had such strong *Provençal* accents that I struggled to understand them. And after so much wine I was having trouble finding my words in English, much less French. Fortunately, whenever I got stuck I would stuff my mouth with food and nod politely, which seemed to work.

After the second dessert it was time for more *eau de vie*, three bottles this time. Then coffee with chocolates.

The lunch had started at noon and we finally made our excuses and left around 7pm. But the party was still going strong.

And they were breaking out the whiskey.

A Night at the Opera

It's important to know who your friends are.

There are many words that are the same in French and English, like nation, pause, and danger. If I don't know a word in French, sometimes I will just fake it by using the English word with a French accent. It works most of the time.

But you have to be careful. There are words that exist in both languages and have entirely different meanings. These are the infamous *faux amis*, or "false friends." Ask Val about the time in Switzerland when she shocked her co-workers by talking about preservatives in food. Oops, *preservative* means "condom."

We should have kept this in mind when we went to the opera.

We were looking at the schedule for the town theater and saw that there was a performance of *La Bohème* coming up, put on by students at a local *collège*. Great, we love opera! And better still, it was free, sponsored by the regional government as part of their arts program.

It was open seating so we got to the theater early. We had to fight our way through the crowd because everyone wanted a good seat. Well before the performance began, every spot was filled and the audience buzzed with anticipation.

The theater darkened and the curtain came up. The opera's opening notes floated over us. Then the singers came onstage and something didn't seem quite right. They were so...young.

Uh oh, wait a minute. *Collège* in French doesn't mean college the way it does in the US. It means something more like middle school. And your average pre-teen isn't yet ready to sing one of Puccini's majestic arias.

So we spent the next hour listening to squeaky voices and off-key notes. We saw Mimi gazing adoringly up at her beloved Rodolfo. Or rather, gazing down, because Mimi towered over poor Rodolfo, who was maybe four feet tall and wearing a jacket several sizes too large.

Despite that, we enjoyed the performance. The

girls' costumes were elegant and the perform-
ers were certainly enthusiastic. You could say
they gave it the old *collège* try! And the audience
loved it, probably because everyone except us
was a relative.

Note to self: double check the dictionary next
time.

Fear the Beard

My beard trimmer broke so I went to buy a new one at the *Intermarché*. I found it on the same aisle that had hair dryers and curling irons and things like that. Except that the beard trimmers were kept in a locked cabinet. *Quoi?*

I tracked down a clerk and asked her to unlock the cabinet so I could get the one I wanted, one that only cost about twenty bucks. She took it out but wouldn't give it to me – no, no, that would not be secure, monsieur! Beard trimmers must follow a special security procedure!

I think it must be like the one for a nuclear weapons factory.

First, I was told to go to the "Special Bureau" at the front of the store. I did that, expecting the lady there to give me the beard trimmer so I could go pay. Oh no, monsieur! That would not be secure! Instead, she gave me a long code to hand to the clerk in the checkout line.

This mystified the poor clerk, who must only deal with women, children and clean-shaven men. But eventually we sorted it out. I paid him and got another piece of paper, this one with a new code, to take back to the Special Bureau.

At this point, I was nervously expecting a retinal scan or maybe a cavity search, but happily I got my beard trimmer.

I asked the lady at the Special Bureau why beard trimmers were kept locked up while the much more expensive hair dryers were not. She looked around carefully, leaned forward and said in a low voice, "Because of the thieves!"

Yes, it seems that beard trimmers were the most-stolen items in *Intermarché* stores nationwide, thus prompting the lockdown. I thanked her for this important news and held the trimmer tightly, scanning the parking lot as I walked carefully to my car.

Later I thought, is this really the best way to deal with the nationwide epidemic of beard trimmer robberies? Is French society well served by having its thieves unable to trim their beards, eventually looking like refugees from a ZZ Top concert? Maybe I should lead the other men in town for a protest march, a very French thing to do.

After trimming my beard, of course.

Vote Early and Often

Val and I agree on most of the important things – politics, which TV shows to watch, the designated hitter rule. But we part ways when it comes to the bread and butter issues.

First it was butter. Val likes the salty kind from Brittany while I like my butter sweet. Agreeing on one butter was a bridge too far, so we finally decided to keep separate butters. It was either that or separate bedrooms.

Now it was baguettes. Should we eat the *baguette de tradition française* or the *talmière*? I'm a traditional kind of guy and preferred the *baguette de tradition*. It is, after all, protected by the French Bread Decree of 1993.

Yes, the French government, concerned about

declining standards, passed a law defining how a proper baguette must be made. There was a sign in our local *boulangerie* certifying that their *baguettes de tradition* "are respectful of" the Bread Decree of 1993.

We had heard rumors of unscrupulous French bakers who had tried to pass off substandard baguettes as true *baguettes de tradition*. They were brought to trial in France's highest court, reserved for only the most serious crimes. Those found guilty were sent to Devil's Island, where they were forced to survive on a diet of bread and water. Most horribly, it was Wonder Bread.

While I liked the traditional baguette, Val had decided she preferred the *talmière*. It was modern, sleek, sexy – like she is. When we walked to the *boulangerie* every morning, she would speed up to try to get in first and place our order, while I would do the same. We finally reached an uneasy truce, alternating the type of baguette we bought.

But that wasn't good enough for Val.

She looked at my plate one day and pointed out accusingly that I hadn't eaten as much bread as she had (only in France would inadequate bread consumption be a crime). "We need proportional voting," she said. "One slice, one vote. And because I eat more bread, I get more votes."

Zut! Her strict Cartesian logic put me in a bind. What to do?

I tried stuffing the ballot box by sneaking slices to Lucca under the table. But Val found out and accused me of voter fraud.

We finally agreed to follow the French election system and have a second round of voting. Our friend Joe, a talented bread maker, would be coming soon for a visit and he could cast the deciding vote. I expected furious campaigning ahead.

What's Up, Doc?

Viviane, Gérard and André came over for a lazy Sunday lunch on the patio. Little did they realize the surprise we had in store for them.

After the first course, we decided it was getting warm enough that we needed some shade. André and I went to look for an umbrella in the underground cellar while Val and Viviane prepared the second course and Gérard had a smoke.

After hunting around in the dim and cramped cellar, we found the umbrella under some chairs. As I wrestled it out, I unfortunately forgot that the ceiling was a foot shorter than me. Which I remembered as soon as I stood up.

After whacking my head and opening a long gash, I stumbled my way to the kitchen. Like any head wound, it bled. A lot. Poor André must have thought he was in a slasher film.

After pressure and ice, the bleeding stopped.

I changed clothes and put on a hat to hide the mess, then we went back to our lunch. After all, there's no reason to let a little mishap get in the way of grilled lamb and fresh asparagus.

That night, I did my best to clean the wound but still felt I should seek medical advice. Luckily, our village doctor had drop-in hours on Monday mornings, so we went early the next day and got in line, saying hello to our fellow villagers.

The visit was different from what I'm used to in the US. The doctor lived above her two-room office and had no staff and very little equipment. When my turn came, the no-nonsense doctor and I discussed in French why I had done such a stupid thing, and then she examined and cleaned the wound.

When she asked why I hadn't come the day before (we didn't know she had an off-hours phone number), I foolishly tried a little humor. I said that I couldn't have done much damage because my head is very hard and quite empty. She gave a grunt that meant somewhere between, "You are not funny and your accent is terrible" and "I can understand about the empty head."

She told me to put Vaseline over the wound twice a day and not wash my hair for a week, which meant I was going to be looking like a 1950s greaser soon. Time to get a bigger hat.

When we were done, the doctor wrote up an invoice and took my money, about 30 dollars. Did I mention that it was different from the US?

Technical Difficulties

We went to the *Course Camarguaise* in St.-Rémy because Val needed another fix of those young men in their tight white pants.

I let Val take the photos. I was looking forward to exciting action shots of man versus bull. But somehow they all turned out to be close-ups that looked like this.

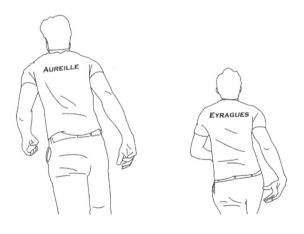

Go With the Flow

I was backing out of a parking spot on the street, a tight one that forced me to go back and forth repeatedly, blocking the road while I did. Val suggested I wait until traffic cleared. "Why?" I said. "After all, we are in France."

Yes, blocking traffic seems to be a national sport in France. It is not uncommon to see a driver stopped in the middle of the road–asking directions, looking at road signs, or perhaps just having a good think about life in general.

I would sometimes see drivers stopped in an intersection, deciding what to do. You would think that they might have looked at a map before leaving home, or maybe they could use a GPS, but what's the fun in that? I once saw someone stopped in a traffic circle while he looked at the signs. Or maybe he was having a chat with his wife about where to have lunch.

Even more surprising was the driver who

missed his exit in a traffic circle, stopped, and backed up to the exit he wanted. Now, I've missed exits myself, but traffic circles are not very big so I just go around again. They are circles, after all. If I'm confused, I may even go around more than once. One time I went around so many times I got dizzy.

But I never had the brilliant idea of backing up into oncoming traffic. That must be because of my inadequate Anglo-Saxon mind. Alas, there is so much still to learn about true Frenchness.

One day I was driving on a busy highway when the car in front of me stopped suddenly to pick up a hitchhiker. Not over on the shoulder, mind you, but in the middle of the highway, while the other drivers screeched to a halt and a traffic jam formed.

The surprising thing is that everyone accepts this. No one ever honks, they just wait patiently while the driver finishes whatever he is doing and starts up again.

So blocking traffic while I got out of my parking place was normal. I felt proud of myself, almost French, like on one of the rare occasions when I actually pronounce something correctly.

Later that day we were on a country road, looking for a winery. The directions were confusing and I had to stop in an intersection to look at the road signs. And the guy behind me honked!

Must have been a New Yorker.

Grease is the Word

I finally got a chance to wash my hair, a week after I cut my head. Thank goodness.

Do you know what happens when you put Vaseline on your head three times a day and don't wash your hair?

- The Department of Energy declares your head part of the nation's Strategic Oil Reserve.
- You look so bad that you wear your hat everywhere, or at least until your wife complains that it is scratching her in bed.
- You become eligible for membership in OPEC.
- Exxon offers to lease the drilling rights to your head.

Good thing I washed my hair, because Val was thinking of signing that deal with Exxon.

He Looks Good in That Dress

One night, Val and I had an extreme cultural experience.

For years we had heard about the Eurovision Song Contest. Every year, dozens of countries each nominate a singer or band that tries to win the award for best pop song.

Eurovision is a very big deal, sort of a cross between American Idol and the Olympics. And it has more viewers than the Super Bowl!

The contest began in the 1950's and notable winners include ABBA. We heard about this repeatedly in the weeks leading up to the finals.

We eventually learned that ABBA was actually the *only* notable winner. As for the others...

we all remember Helena Paparizou and Marija Šerifović, don't we?

The reputation of Eurovision was that some acts would be terrific, some would be cheesy, and some a combination of both.

We were not disappointed.

Twenty-six countries were in the finals, from mighty Germany to tiny San Marino.Everyone sang in English.

Well, almost everyone. Who didn't? That would be the French, who were rewarded for their linguistic loyalty by finishing dead last.

The Swiss were true to form – straightforward, efficient and boring. And fortunately no yodeling.

But let's get to the good part – the cheese.

The Azerbaijan contestant must have needed something to distract us from her not-so-great voice because while she sang, another lady cavorted on a trapeze.

Montenegro took the same approach, but this time it was an ice skater gliding around onstage.

And the Iceland boy band sang while bouncing up and down on a trampoline.

My favorite was Ukraine. Their entrant sang a catchy tune while a guy ran around inside a giant hamster wheel.

I figured the hamster wheel was the peak of cheesiness until Austria came up. Their entrant called himself the Bearded Lady. But not like in an old circus act. No, this was a dude with long hair, mascara, false eyelashes, a sparkly evening gown...and a full beard.

Total cheese!

Then he started singing. He turned out to have a lovely voice. And his song was catchy. I could see Val tapping her foot and nodding her head with the beat. My god, could he actually win?

When the votes were tallied it wasn't even close – the Bearded Lady was the runaway winner.

And definitely more memorable than Marija Šerifović.

Our Local Costco

We were lucky to have several outdoor markets near us.

Our village had two market days, Wednesday and Saturday mornings. On Wednesday there were just a few vendors, like the fish truck, the cheese truck, and the fruit and vegetable man. And, of course, there were roast chickens and paella. All of the essentials were covered.

Saturday's market was bigger, with more vendors plus clothing and flower stands. I liked to get a coffee and a croissant and read *Le Monde* while Val went shopping. I'd become a regular at the local café. The owner would see me coming up the street and have my coffee ready by the time I sat down.

Then there was what we thought of as our local Costco. It was the *Marché des Producteurs* in Velleron, the next town over. It was open every evening except Sunday and was not touristy at all, just a big parking lot where farmers brought their produce to sell direct.

The farmers parked their trucks and vans in two long lines and sold right out of the back, with only fold-up tables for their goods. One stand might have strawberries and apricots. Another zucchini. One lady specialized in chickpeas and made all kinds of hummus.

There were more than a hundred vendors and the lot quickly filled with people. The market was so busy that the town had to post two cops to direct traffic. A rickety bar opened its doors each night to serve the thirsty shoppers.

Because it was an evening market, it meant that the fruit and vegetables had been picked that day. You could buy just one or you could get a whole crate. And the prices were incredible; sometimes we felt like we were stealing. One night we bought two pounds of cherries for $2.50. They were so sweet they tasted like candy.

Say It Ain't So, Joe

We had the pleasure of hosting our friend Joe the baker. It was his first time in Provence so it gave us the opportunity to show him around our favorite places.

Joe also helped us resolve our bread and butter issues. You may recall that Val prefers the *talmière* style of baguette while I am a staunch supporter of the *baguette de tradition*. And Val is a fan of salty butter while I like my butter sweet. We decided to let Joe be the tiebreaker.

Happily, he agreed with me about the sweet butter, while showing proper distain for the salty. But I am sorry to say that Joe turned out to be a *talmière* kind of guy. So much for male solidarity.

The Key to French Greatness

We Americans love our peanut butter, just like Australians love Vegemite and Brits love Marmite. We all have our national favorites.

For the French it is Nutella, that sweet chocolate-hazelnut spread that kids grow up eating at breakfast.

So it was shocking when French philosopher Régis Debray attacked Nutella, causing a national uproar. He might as well have gone after Motherhood and the 35-hour workweek while he was at it.

The background was a proposed set of educational reforms, including a de-emphasis on the teaching of Latin and other traditional subjects. Debray felt that these changes would make school too easy.

He chose to express his view this way, "Civilization is not Nutella, it is Effort!" Cue the gasps.

Mara Goyet responded in *Le Monde* with an essay explaining the ways in which Nutella is, in fact, at the very heart of French civilization. Not only was the essay funny, it was an excellent example of the art of *débat* that the French love so much.

My translation is below.

Régis Debray Knows Nothing About Nutella

Régis Debray has said, "Civilization is not Nutella, it is Effort!" One feels that the school reform debate has now reached its summit. The image is strong, profound, grandiose. But, unfortunately, it is wrong. Nutella IS effort.

Why?

Because it is practically impossible to stop eating. Every day, Nutella is a battle against oneself, against one's impulses, against one's own excesses. Nutella is a form of spiritual exercise, the fight against the demon of piggishness. It is therefore an art of self-mastery.

Because it demands, after eating, long efforts to lose

weight. We learn to measure the consequences of our actions.

Because it requires that we clean the knife and the spoon by hand. Thanks to Nutella, the young learn the traditional gestures from their grandmothers, which modernity might otherwise cause us to lose. It is a link between generations, a vector of tradition.

Because it is difficult to get its damned lid off. And it is difficult to scrape out the last bits from the jar. Like learning Greek, it requires us to delay the moment of satisfaction. It refuses the "Now Now Now."

Because one NEVER puts it in the refrigerator. Nutella is proof of resistance, eternity, sang-froid. It refuses the diktat of the consume-by date. It commits for the duration—it is devilishly Braudélian.

Because once you eat Nutella, you really don't want to eat anything else. It does not participate in the civilization of channel surfing. One learns to concentrate on one object, simple and unique, without dissipating one's energies.

In sum, it is inappropriate for Monsieur Debray to exclaim on a subject as grave as Nutella without understanding it. Education policy, perhaps. But Nutella, no, never Nutella.

Channel Surfing

We weren't sure what to watch on TV so we checked the guide.

We were thrilled to see that the top prize-winner of a recent Cannes Film Festival was showing that night. Cannes is an important French cultural event and the *Palme d'Or* is one of France's most prestigious awards.

We figured that any film that won that prize must be fun to watch. And it would be good for our French. Even if we didn't understand every word, we could at least follow the action.

Then we saw that it was three and a half hours long.

And the description read, "This masterpiece is a philosophical talkfest about life and death, good and evil, the beauty of the world and the art of conversation."

We decided to watch the news.

Merci

We were walking through town with Lucca when an older gentleman asked what breed of dog he was. We stopped to talk and he quickly figured out from our accents that we are not native French speakers.

"Are you English?" he asked suspiciously. Relations across the English Channel are not always the friendliest.

His frown became a smile when we explained that we are Americans. He shook our hands warmly and thanked us for "saving" France in 1944.

It wasn't the first time this had happened. It was always gratifying to know that American sacrifices during the war are still remembered and honored.

When someone thanked us for 1944 we always tried to return the favor.

We would express our gratitude for France's essential support during our war of independence. We would point out that France is America's oldest ally.

And we would tell them something that even most Americans don't know.

There are only two portraits in the House of Representatives, one of the centers of American government. These large paintings hold pride of place, flanking the Speaker's rostrum. On the left is the father of our country, George Washington; on the right, French general Lafayette.

And the painting of Lafayette came first.

La Mer

Marie-France and Xavier invited us to join them for lunch at a restaurant in Niolon, a tiny port town on the Mediterranean coast. Sophie and Jacques came as well and we climbed into two cars for the drive down.

I drove one car, with Xavier and Marie-France, which meant I got a private French lesson. Marie-France was really interested in the US university system and kept asking me questions. How do college admissions work? Why does it cost so much? Do students take classes in football?

Trying to concentrate on French and concentrate on driving at the same time was not a good idea. Happily, after a couple of near misses, we arrived safely.

We ate at a place right on the port, where the fish had been caught that morning. The outline of Marseille, topped by its famous Notre Dame basilica, was visible a few miles down the rocky coast. It was so perfect I felt like we had stepped into a brochure from the Tourism Promotion Board.

After lunch we went for a hike in the hills above town, then drove back to Sophie and Jacques's place for a long *aperitif*. It was a pleasure to be together with our new friends, drinking wine and eating little snacks.

The conversation was wide-ranging – French history, Buddhist philosophy, stone-carving techniques. I was able to follow most of it and add in my two cents from time to time. What a difference from our first stay in Provence! Back then I sometimes couldn't even tell what subject was being discussed.

When we finally arrived home, we realized the entire day had been in French, including discussions of some complicated subjects. It was great for our French learning, but also exhausting, and we were both spent.

I was so mentally empty that I felt like someone had scrubbed out the inside of my head with steel wool. I can't remember another time my brain was so blank.

We started to talk about our plans for the next day but had trouble forming sentences. So we stared at each other for a while, then at the walls, before finally giving up and going to bed.

Good Sports

It was Sophie and Jacques's wedding anniversary so we brought them a bouquet of flowers. We don't usually help our friends celebrate an anniversary but we had become close to Sophie and Jacques in a surprisingly short amount of time.

They invited us to stay and watch TV together. It was the finals of the French Open tennis tournament, known in France by the name of the stadium where it is played, *Roland Garros*. Jacques is a huge sports fan and he especially loves tennis.

We sat together and watched the match, chatting the whole time. We would remark when a player made an especially good or bad shot. Jacques would explain a player's tendencies or how the weather was affecting play. Sometimes I would ask a question and Jacques would help me understand what was going on.

After a while I was startled to realize that hours had gone by and we had been speaking French the whole time. We weren't having much of a conversation so it didn't demand anything complicated. But it was the first time that I had been "in French" for so long *and not even realized it.*

It felt like a breakthrough and I was thrilled because I had been working toward it for years. All those hours conjugating verbs and memorizing vocabulary had led to this. However imperfectly, I could *communicate!* Yes!

Another thing that struck me was that the afternoon felt no different than if we had been doing the same thing in California, hanging out with friends and watching sports on TV. Although instead of having nachos and beer, we were enjoying champagne and French pastries that Sophie had made that morning.

Ok, so maybe it was a little different.

My Final French Exam

"Have you ever had sex with a man?"

The doctor waited for my answer, staring grimly at me. Sweat trickled down my forehead as I tried to make sure I had understood her correctly. My French was getting better but this certainly wasn't a question that had ever come up in class.

I knew that if I got it wrong I'd be in big trouble. Finally I was ready.

"*Non.*"

The doctor moved on to the next question. Whew, got that one right!

I was being interviewed before donating blood and I was nervous. Some years ago, tainted blood had gotten into the French blood supply, causing people to die of AIDS. So today the French are extra cautious. In addition to the usual blood tests, every person who donates has to be interviewed privately by a doctor as a precaution.

When we had been in France the last time, I had tried to donate but my French hadn't been strong enough for the interview. The doctor rejected my blood due to "insufficient command of the French language" (that's got to be a first.) So I considered this interview as kind of a final exam.

There were two doctors doing the interviewing, a friendly one and her evil twin.

Val, of course, got the friendly doctor. I could hear them chatting and laughing in the next room. By the end I think they were exchanging recipes for *ratatouille.*

By contrast, my interview was more like the Inquisition. My doctor was humorless and aggressive, asking question after question at a rapid fire pace. If I answered a single one wrong, I would be done for.

"Have you ever had a skin graft?"

"Have you ever had brain surgery?"

"Why did the Forty-Niners waste a first-round draft pick on a wide receiver?"

Ok, I made that last one up. But everyone knows the team needs help on the defensive line.

The questions came faster and faster. I was really sweating now. Finally, after more than a dozen questions, it looked like I might be ok. There was just one last thing. The doctor grinned fiendishly.

"Give me your wrist."

Ahhh! I just about jumped out of my chair. I thought she was going to put me on the rack or something. But no, she just had to check my blood pressure. Luckily, it's always nice and low. Unless someone is making me nervous...

"*Non!* It is a tiny bit too high! You are rejected!" She slammed my file shut.

Putain! Rejected again! However...

Super! I passed my French exam! Even if the examiner was a real *connasse*.

On the Road Again

Once again, springtime came to an end and once again we drove north to Frankfurt. We reflected on our stay and how far we had come over the last few years.

Our first trip had been pretty basic–we were just trying to figure out how to live several months a year in France. Could we manage it? While we had stumbled along the way and embarrassed ourselves plenty of times, happily the answer had been yes.

On our second trip we had discovered language partners. It was like finding a secret door into France. They had helped us, and especially me, make progress in the language. Even better, our partners had become our friends and we had begun to develop a social life.

This third time had been different. We felt like we had been able to connect on a much deeper level than before.

Unlike our previous stays, where we had lived

outside of small towns, this time we had lived in a town itself. We had gotten to know our neighbors, shopped at the outdoor market every week, and become regulars at the café. We had developed a circle of friends that we saw regularly, for bike rides or meals or just an *aperitif.*

These friends had introduced us, in turn, to their friends. And even if we didn't know them well, we knew their names and would wave or say hello when we saw them in town. To be able to walk through *centre ville* and see a friendly face made us feel connected to the town and the people in it. We hadn't become locals but we no longer felt like the foreigners we had been at the start.

We weren't just spectators anymore, observing the lovable eccentricities of the French. Now we were part of the show ourselves, doing our best to become regular (and in our own way, eccentric) participants in the daily life of this little corner of Provence.

We were gradually building a life in France to complement the one we had in the US.

And it is a project that is far from finished.

Acknowledgements

I would first like to thank my friend George Anders, the Pulitzer Prize-winning journalist and best-selling author, for all of his help and support. I would not have begun this book without his encouragement.

I would like to thank the friends who critiqued the various manuscripts as this book developed: Jeff Britting, Joe Doniach, Elizabeth Mori and Shu Ann Stidolph. Their thoughtful comments were invaluable. Elizabeth had a knack for pointing out the many things I had done wrong in a friendly and positive way, greatly improving the book. And Jeff helped me see how I could share my French journey with readers in a more personal, and better, way.

I would like to thank my French teachers Gisèle Filiol, Marjorie Hamelin and Malika Labidi for helping me make progress in the beautiful language of Molière. I promise them that someday

I will finally get the subjunctive tense right. And a shout-out to my classmates for their patience as I struggled to keep up with them.

To my French friends, who make part-time living in France so delicious, I say *Merci bien, chers bons amis.*

And first, last and always, I would like to thank my beloved wife Val, without whom this adventure would never have been possible.

Resources

LANGUAGE PARTNERS

A great resource for finding language partners is www.mylanguageexchange.com. It allows you to search for a potential partner, specifying parameters such as your native language, your target language, and the gender and age range of the language partner you are seeking. You can also choose whether you want to exchange by email, text, voice, or even face-to-face. You can then review profiles of the candidate partners that the search turns up. You, in turn, add your own profile. In these brief profiles, users write about themselves, describing things like their language goals, their level of proficiency, and their hobbies.

LANGUAGE RESOURCES

An excellent resource for both French language and French culture is www.commeunefrancaise.

com. The delightful French host, Géraldine Lepere, gives a weekly video lesson on subjects like "Favorite French Expressions," "5 Embarrassing Mistakes in French" and "How to Order Coffee in France Like a Local." Much of the material is free and she also offers paid courses in French language and customs.

A very helpful resource for learning French is www.learnfrenchbypodcast.com. It offers short audio lessons composed of a dialog about an interesting topic, an explanation of some of the words and expressions used, and a quiz. The audios are free and the accompanying written materials cost just a dollar per lesson. I did these with a friend and found that listening to the dialog, then reading it out loud back and forth really helped improve my pronunciation.

For intensive grammar study, which I hate (who doesn't?), www.kwiziq.com is very good. Kwiziq has a system of short quizzes that drill you on grammar, with daily reminders and progress charts. The content of each quiz is based on your prior results, so you are constantly focusing on the things you need to work on. It makes the dull task of grammar study almost fun, which is saying a lot. You can take ten quizzes a month for free and need to buy a subscription to take more. An annual subscription is about $150 but you can also subscribe on a monthly basis.

French Word-A-Day (www.french-word-a-day.typepad.com) is an excellent resource for learning French customs, words and phrases, especially those that don't show up in your typical French course. The author Kristi Espinasse is also the author of the charming book <u>Words in a French Life</u>.

And, of course, I never leave home without the Larousse French-English dictionary on my phone (about $5 in your favorite App Store).

TV, MAGAZINES AND PODCASTS

Le Monde (www.lemonde.fr) is the leading French newspaper. It is easier to read than you might think because it uses straightforward language and hardly any slang. I like to read about something in the US press, then read about the same thing in Le Monde. This helps me understand the French article more easily, plus it gives me a different perspective on the news. Le Monde has a wide variety of digital offerings ranging from free to about $5 per month to pretty expensive.

TV5 Monde is a French television station you may be able subscribe to with your cable package. I pay about $10 a month for it. It's a good way to hear French spoken, whether it's the news or the weather report or one of their many TV programs. They also offer a good online French learning program (www.apprendre.tv5monde.com).

French Morning (www.frenchmorning.com) is a free daily electronic newsletter about current events in the US that have a French connection. It offers both French and English-language editions.

France Today (www.francetoday.com) is an English-language magazine with excellent articles on things to see and do in France. It comes in both print and digital editions.

France-Amérique (www.france-amerique.com) is an interesting bilingual magazine focusing on all things French, such as history, culture, business, and food.

There is a seemingly unlimited supply of pod-casts in French. Some of my favorites are *Le marche de l'histoire, Les Aventuriers de l'impossible, La Tête au carré* and *Les Hommes aux semelles de vent.*

TRAVEL

For a long-term stay in France, renting a car can be brutally expensive. So the French came up with an answer. It's a program for long-term rentals offered only to foreigners and supported by all the French auto manufacturers (Peugeot, Renault, and Citroen.) Technically, you buy the car at the beginning and sell it back at the end, but it comes with 100% insurance so you don't take any risk. You even get a new car, which you pick yourself! And an automatic transmission doesn't cost much more than a manual. Note that it helps to book well ahead of time. The rule of thumb is that this program is cheaper than renting if your trip is longer than three weeks. Kemwel (www.kemwel.com) is a terrific company to work with to get a car this way.

To find a long-term rental house, I have used

websites like Abritel (www.abritel.fr), Homelidays (www.homelidays.com) and VRBO (www.vrbo.com). All of these have now been acquired by HomeAway (www.homeaway.com) so I usually just look there, although the various websites may still have slight differences between them. Airbnb (www.airbnb.com) is another option, though is usually focused more on short-term rentals.

Angloinfo (www.angloinfo.com) is a website for English-speakers in France. It provides information on resources (plumbers, hairdressers, computer repair, etc.), plus upcoming events in your area, discussion boards, classified ads, and more.

Last, the local tourist office (*Office de Tourisme*) is usually a great resource, with information about just about anything you could need, including rental housing. I am surprised by how often even small towns have their own tourist office, so if yours doesn't have one, try the next town over.

Meet The Author

Keith Van Sickle is the author of the Amazon best-seller *One Sip at a Time: Learning to Live in Provence* and its sequel *Are We French Yet? Keith & Val's Adventures in Provence.* A lifelong traveler who got his first taste of overseas life as a university student in England, Keith later backpacked around the world on his own. But it was the expat assignment to Switzerland that made him fall in love with Europe. With his wife Val and their trusty dog Mica, he now splits his time between California and Provence, delving ever deeper into what makes France so endlessly fascinating.

Keep up with Keith online:

Website: https://keithvansickle.com
Facebook: Keith Van Sickle, Author
Twitter: @keith_vansickle

Read on for a sneak peek at *Are We French Yet?*...

Not Quite What I Planned

Val and I couldn't wait to get back to France. For weeks, we had been packing our bags and cleaning our house in preparation for our three-month trip abroad. Getting ready for springtime in Provence is a complicated affair, and even though we've done it many times, it never gets easier.

Finally, just three days before our flight, we'd worked through most of our long checklist and had some free time on our hands. Whenever we are about to go on a long trip like this I get nervous—not the worried kind of nervous but rather the excited-and-can't-wait-to-get-going kind of nervous. I started pacing around the house.

"You look like you need something to do," said Val. "Let's go for a bike ride out on Old Page Mill Road. We can get some exercise before we have to sit on a plane all day."

"Good idea!" I said. Except it wasn't.

We like to ride on Old Page Mill because it's a quiet road with hardly any cars. It's shady and has gentle hills, which is perfect for us because we're not serious bikers. In fact, we're kind of slow. I can't count the times I've been passed by riders on expensive bikes, wearing their sleek outfits, while I poke along in my baggy shorts and old polo shirt.

It was a quiet day so I let my mind wander as we pedaled along. Val sometimes accuses me of being, um, inattentive, and this time she was definitely right. I started thinking about what to have for dinner when we got to France—should it be *coq au vin* or *daube de boeuf*? No, I thought, I'll have my favorite, *confit de canard*.

I was dreamily savoring that first bite of crispy duck when a squirrel darted in front of me. I didn't see it until it was too late and I slammed on the brakes, which only made a bad situation worse. The front tire locked up and I went flying over the handlebars. The next thing I knew I was lying on the ground and my right wrist hurt. A lot.

Val ran over to me. "Are you ok?" she said, a panicked look on her face.

"I'm still in one piece," I said, "but my wrist really hurts. I think we'd better go to the hospital."

We spent the rest of the afternoon in the emergency room, waiting our turn while my wrist throbbed and I worried about our trip to Provence. Would we have to cancel it? We had already paid for our flight and rental car, plus the house we would be staying in for three months. If I couldn't travel, could we get our money back?

Then there was medical care. Would I be able to get what I needed in France? What about physical therapy? And would our insurance pay for it?

Even if we could still go to France, I wouldn't be 100% when we got there. I hadn't hurt my legs so I could still walk, but if my wrist was broken would I be able to drive?

You have a lot of time to fret when you're in a waiting room.

A nurse eventually called my name and X-rays confirmed the worst—a broken wrist that would take two months to heal. Next I saw a doctor who put a cast on my hand and lower arm and told me to come back in a month for a checkup.

"I'm sorry," I said, "but I can't because I'll be in France then."

"That's fine," he said, "French doctors are excellent. Just make an appointment with a hand specialist there. And be sure to do physical therapy after the bone heals."

"Right," I thought, "like that's going to be easy." I didn't know much about the French health care system, so finding a specialized doctor and therapist was a daunting challenge. This definitely wasn't the fun start to our trip that I had been hoping for.

The Interrogation

Three days after I broke my wrist, Val and I set off for France with our suitcases plus our dog and her crate. Schlepping all that gear is tough enough without a broken bone and here I was one-armed and practically useless (or as Val would say, "More useless than usual.")

Luckily, a friend drove us to the airport and helped carry our bags to the check-in counter. And Val had the presence of mind to reserve a porter to help us when our flight landed in Europe. But she still had to do most of the work and hasn't let me forget it. She claims that it gave her "brownie points for life" and she gleefully redeems them whenever she gets the chance.

Once we settled into our place in Provence, it was time to track down that doctor.

"How do I find one?" I asked Val. "They don't have Yellow Pages here. And what do you even call somebody like that?" It's not like "hand specialist" was in our French dictionary (I checked).

"Let's ask Sophie," suggested Val. "She always knows what to do."

That was a good idea. Sophie and her husband Jacques are friends of ours so I called her, making sure to look up a few words first so I could explain what had happened. You never know when you'll have the opportunity to expand your vocabulary and this time it was *percuter* (to crash), *cassé* (broken) and *radius* (radius bone).

Sophie, as always, came to the rescue. By the next day she had found a hand specialist at a nearby clinic and made an appointment for me. The clinic was called *SOS Main* (SOS Hand), which didn't sound very medical to me— it sounded more like what you use to wave in distress. Not sure what to expect, Val decided to join me and off to the clinic we went.

We arrived well before my appointment and it was a good thing we did because I was told I needed a French X-ray. I had brought the one taken in the US but for some reason it wasn't good enough, so I was sent downstairs to the X-ray center where I waited in line with about a dozen other people. When it was finally my turn I tried to be helpful and told the technician that I had *cassé le fin de mon radius* (broken the end of my radius bone), pointing to where the break was.

She looked at me like I was a two-year-old. *"Ce n'est pas le fin du radius, c'est l'extrémité,"* she said (It's not the *end* of the radius bone, it's the *extremity*).

"Sheesh," I thought, "is there really such a big difference?" I was reminded yet again how precise the French are with their language.

After the X-ray, Val and I headed up for my appointment with the doctor. It did not start well.

In the US, back in the old days, doctors were kind of like gods. They told you what to do and you did it. You never questioned a doctor and you certainly didn't suggest treatments based on your Internet research or something your neighbor told you. It's still like that in France— Me Important Doctor, you lowly patient.

The doctor introduced himself as Dr. Selemi and formally shook hands with us because the French just love to shake hands. My handshake was awkward and left-handed due to my broken right wrist but it was important that we follow protocol. Then the doctor started aggressively asking me questions in French. I would barely start to answer one question and he would launch into another.

"When was your accident? No, *exactly* when?"

"How did this happen?"

"Why didn't you avoid the squirrel? They are quite small, you know."

"Why didn't you have surgery? I would have operated on your wrist immediately. What's wrong with your American doctor?"

After I answered his questions in a suitably deferential fashion and showed that I could sort of speak French, the doctor started to mellow. Then he threw me a curveball.

"How many states have you visited in America?"

Where did that come from? I was so startled by the question that it took me a moment to answer. "Uh...er...um...maybe half," I finally stammered.

"I've been to 43!" he said proudly.

To my surprise, I learned that Dr. Selemi is a huge fan of the US. He fell in love with the country as a high school exchange student and now vacations there every year. AND he speaks English way better than I speak French. So I could have avoided a lot of heartburn if he had just conducted his interrogation in English.

I must have passed his test because he suddenly became very friendly. The French can be formal and even aloof at first but we got past that quickly. We started chatting and I asked if he had ever visited my home state of California.

"Of course," he said. "I've been to Disneyland, Yosemite, San Francisco, and lots of other places. My favorite is Napa Valley because I love wine."

"Oh, me too," I said, "and the ones from around here are my favorites."

"Really?" he said, then paused and looked thoughtful for a moment. "Well you know, I have a friend..."

It turns out that this friend owns a winery in nearby Châteauneuf-du-Pape, one of the most famous wine towns in the world. Dr. Selemi excused himself to make a phone call and the next thing we knew we were invited to a private tasting on the following Sunday.

This was one of those "Toto, I don't think we're in Kansas any more" moments. Somehow, some way, in just a few minutes I'd gone from being an idiot who couldn't avoid an itty-bitty squirrel to being invited to a famous winery. With a doctor I'd just met!

As we drove home after the appointment, Val looked at me and said, "This would *never* happen back home."

Doctor's Orders

Châteauneuf-du-Pape means "the Pope's new chateau" because his summer palace had once been there. This was back in the 14th century, when the papacy moved from Rome to nearby Avignon for about a hundred years. The ruins of the famous chateau still tower over the countryside, surrounded by mile after mile of what had once been papal vineyards. It was early spring on the day of our wine tasting and the vines were beginning to bud, creating a sea of bright green in all directions.

We were allowed to bring two friends so we invited Sophie and Jacques—he's one of my wine buddies and was thrilled because it's not every day you get a private tasting at a top *domaine*. On Sunday morning, church bells ringing, we all met in the town's main square.

"Dr. Selemi," I said, "I'd like to introduce you to Sophie and Jacques."

"Oh please, call me Elyas," he said, shaking their hands. "There's no reason to be stuffy." So now we were on a first-name basis!

It was a beautiful day—the sky was blue, the air was crisp and we were ready to taste some seriously good wine. By luck, that day was also the town's annual wine fair and Elyas had generously bought us tickets.

The fair was held in the town's community center, a big, plain room that you could imagine being used for Bingo games on a Tuesday night. But now it was filled with row after row of foldup tables. Every winemaker in town was there, each of them standing behind a table covered with bottles of wine, while people milled around in the aisles. All you had to do was walk up to a table and stick out your glass for a pour of some of the best wine in the world. The whole affair was informal and friendly, not a wine snob in sight.

"I think I'm in heaven," said Jacques.

"Thank goodness," I said, "that I can still drink wine with my left hand!"

As we worked our way through the room, swirling and sipping, Elyas kept making introductions—to his family, his friends, his friends' friends, winemakers he knew, people from the village, it went on and on. After a couple of hours, our heads were spinning from all that sipping and we decided to break for lunch. We went to the food hall where Elyas introduced us to Françoise, the owner of the winery and the host of our private tasting. We all chatted together over lunch and when it was over, Elyas surprised us by deciding to go home.

"I've had enough wine for today and need to stop," he said. "Doctor's orders!"

That left the four of us with Françoise, who was not only the owner of the winery—the seventh generation in her family—but also its chief winemaker and the president of the local women's winemaking association. She was talented and accomplished and remarkably generous with her time, spending hours with us, people she barely knew.

First she drove us to her winery outside of town, where she gave us a tour and an explanation of every step of the winemaking process. We saw the places where her workers brought in the grapes, sorted them, crushed them, separated out the juice and let it ferment into wine, then bottled it and shipped it to customers around the world. The best part was when she took us down to the cellar to taste some young wine. The *cave* was chilly and dark.

Françoise turned a tap on one of the gigantic barrels and filled a glass. "Here," she said, "try this and tell me what you think."

What did I think? I thought it was dark and delicious and a bit mysterious because it was still evolving. We went from one barrel to the next, tasting the wine from each and comparing them. Françoise tasted along with us, explaining how she planned to take a little of this one and a little of that one to come up with the perfect blend for the next year's wines.

Jacques and I had visited wineries before but never received the royal treatment like this. It was a kind of master class in winemaking and we were such enthusiastic students that I think Françoise enjoyed it as much as we did.

After the winery tour, we went back to her tasting room in town to try more wines, older ones, and Françoise explained to us how they changed over time.

Finally—late afternoon now—it was time to say our goodbyes. We had shaken hands when first introduced, but our time together had somehow broken down a barrier so now it was kisses on the cheek all around, left-right-left in the local style. As Sophie, Jacques, Val and I walked contentedly, if a bit unsteadily, back to our cars, we marveled at what a magical day it had been.

Magical, that's the right word. Magic seems to happen to us in France.

Praise For Are We French Yet?

"Return to the enticing landscapes of Provence as Keith and Val continue their adventure of expat living. Each chapter is an entertaining vignette that combines Keith's warm humour with insightful observations and candid experiences. On y va!"
–Patricia Sands, author of *The First Noël and Love in Provence*

"A romp through Provence replete with food, fun, and friendship. Next best thing to being there!"
–K. S. R. Burns, author of *The Paris Effect and Paris Ever After*

"Full of hilarity and nostalgia, Are We French Yet? gives us the inside scoop on what life is really like in Provence"
–*Backyard Provence*

"Keith transports the reader into everyday experiences in his lighthearted and breezy recounts of French strikes, muzzle salad, and the strict etiquette for entering a doctor's office"
—*A French Collection*

"It's the journey to becoming French that counts and while it hasn't been easy for Keith and Val, what a ride!"
—*France Travel Tips*

"An enjoyable read and a look at French customs with an open and curious mind"
—*Perfectly Provence*

Available from Amazon

Made in the USA
Columbia, SC
07 August 2021

43153851R00115